THE
KITCHEN PANTRY
SCIENTIST

BIOLOGY
FOR KIDS

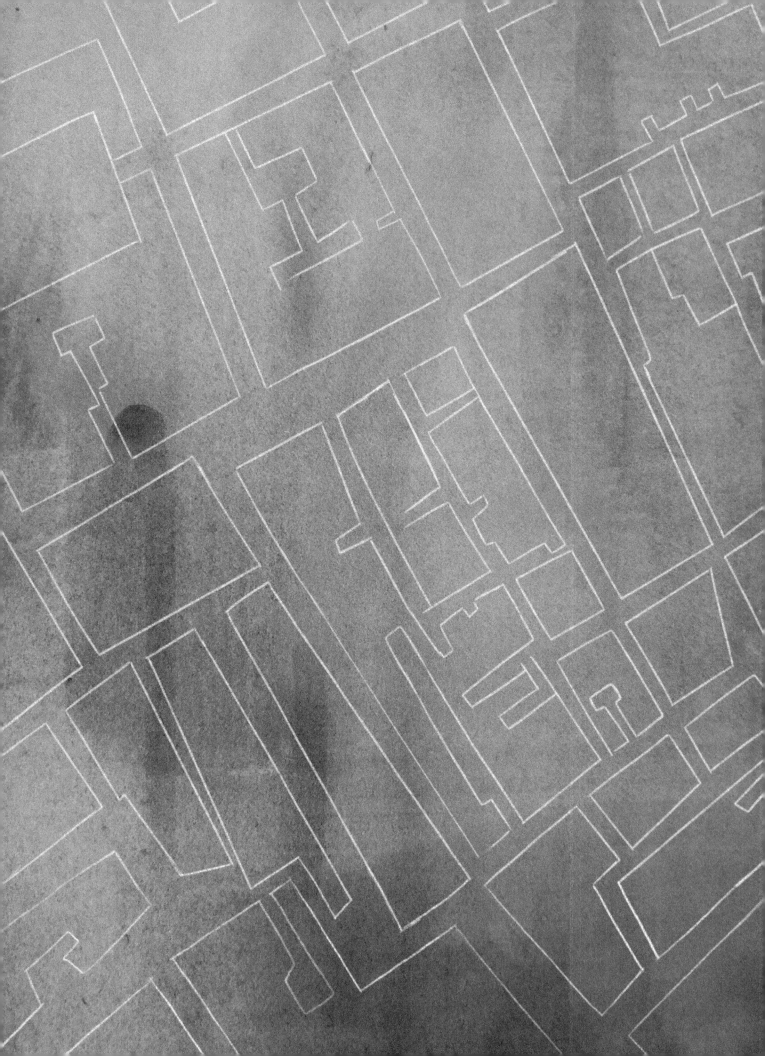

THE

KITCHEN PANTRY

SCIENTIST

BIOLOGY
FOR KIDS

Science EXPERIMENTS AND ACTIVITIES Inspired
by AWESOME BIOLOGISTS, Past and Present

LIZ LEE HEINECKE

QUARRY

Quarto.com

© 2021 Quarto Publishing Group USA Inc.
Text © 2021 Liz Lee Heinecke

First Published in 2021 by Quarry Books,
an imprint of The Quarto Group,
100 Cummings Center, Suite 265-D, Beverly, MA 01915, USA.
T (978) 282-9590 F (978) 283-2742

Quarry Books titles are also available at discount
for retail, wholesale, promotional, and bulk purchase.
For details, contact the Special Sales Manager by email at
specialsales@quarto.com or by mail at The Quarto Group,
Attn: Special Sales Manager, 100 Cummings Center,
Suite 265-D, Beverly, MA 01915, USA.

ISBN: 978-1-63159-832-6

Digital edition published in 2021
eISBN: 978-1-63159-833-3

Library of Congress Cataloging-in-Publication Data available.

Design: Debbie Berne
Cover Illustrations: Kelly Anne Dalton
Illustration of author: Mattie Wells (cover and page 3)
Page Layout: Debbie Berne
Photography: Amber Procaccini Photography
Illustration: Kelly Anne Dalton

THIS BOOK IS DEDICATED
TO WOMEN OF COLOR IN SCIENCE
AND MEDICINE.

CONTENTS

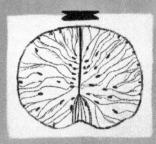

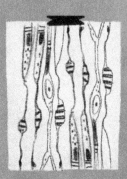

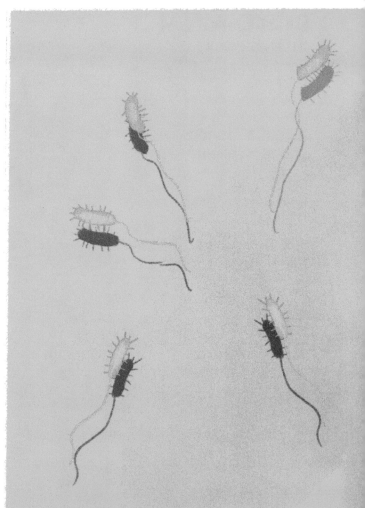

INTRODUCTION

With a few simple ingredients, you can bring science history to life. Table salt, water, and a raw egg are all you need to try an experiment once performed by Charles Darwin to test whether bird and reptile eggs could float from South America to the Galápagos Islands. Recycle a cardboard tube to see with your own eyes how Patricia Bath's innovations in cataract surgery restored the vision of millions of people. Grow microbes on agar medium to learn how Frannie Hess's idea revolutionized microbiology. Transform jars, apple juice, and straws into simple versions of swan-necked flasks to replicate one of Louis Pasteur's most famous experiments.

Biology for Kids takes you on a hands-on journey through the lives and work of twenty-five fascinating biologists, past and present. These scientists are a small sampling of the large, diverse group of people who study biology, the science of life. Following each scientist's story, a lab will guide you through an experiment or project based on a concept related to their work.

Long before the word biologist was coined, people around the world realized that by studying the world around them, they could improve their lives. Learning about plants and insects helped them discover new medicines and grow better crops. Studying animals taught them how to raise healthy cattle, horses, and poultry for food or transportation.

Eventually, some famous scientists appeared on the scene and the field of biology started to take shape. In ancient Greece, Hippocrates established medicine as a profession and Aristotle and Theophrastus wrote books about plants and animals. An Iranian botanist and astronomer named Al-Dinawari published a six-volume book of plants.

Around 1670, a Dutchman named Anton van Leeuwenhoek put together the first microscope and called the creatures he saw moving in a drop of pond water "animalcules." His invention helped scientists understand that all living thing are made up of individual units called cells and the field of biology exploded with new ideas.

The variety of life on Earth, which scientists call diversity, is astonishing. In addition to plants and animals, microbes too small to see without a microscope are everywhere: in the air, the soil, the water, and even our bodies. As living things grow in communities, they claim space, gather what they need for survival, and reproduce. Living organisms often cooperate with their neighbors in return for longer, healthier lives. Some trees partner with mushrooms in the soil at their roots. Certain termites grow special fungal gardens, which helps them to digest the wood they eat. Humans depend on the microbes inside of our bodies for survival.

Today's biologists study everything imaginable. From oceans, jungles, and cities to the space station—the universe is their laboratory and there are countless branches of biology to explore. Some biologists map coral reefs or study how animals are changing their behavior as humans move into their territories. Others sequence deoxyribonucleic acid (DNA) or search for ways to improve human health. Building on past discoveries, modern biology propels us forward to new frontiers of understanding.

Whether you hope to be a microbiologist, a shark scientist, or an artist one day, I hope that *Biology for Kids* will help you to appreciate the living things around you.

Maria Sibylla Merian b. 1647
BIOLOGICAL ILLUSTRATION/METAMORPHOSIS

AN ARTIST

Maria Sibylla Merian was born in Germany in 1647. She was encouraged to paint and draw by her stepfather, an artist, who specialized in painting flowers. At that time, women didn't pursue the study of nature, but painting, drawing, and embroidery were considered acceptable hobbies for girls. Maria proved exceptionally talented at drawing the plants and insects she collected.

A NATURALIST

A curious child, Maria started investigating insects when she was young. Her life took a new turn when, at thirteen years old, she learned to raise silkworms. As she observed their metamorphosis from caterpillar to moth, she wrote, "I realized that other caterpillars produced beautiful butterflies or moths, and that silkworms did the same. This led me to collect all the caterpillars I could find in order to see how they changed."

METAMORPHOSIS

Maria married and had children, but she continued to paint. Besides teaching other young women to draw, she learned to make copperplate engravings of her illustrations so that they could be printed on paper. It was important to Maria that she accurately represent the color of the plants, insects, and spiders in her work, so she hand-colored many of the prints she made herself.

CATERPILLARS

After years of work, Maria published two volumes of stunning illustrations of the life cycles of the caterpillars she'd studied. Other artists had drawn butterflies before, but she was the first to accurately depict their entire life cycles, including where butterflies and moths laid their eggs, which plants certain caterpillars ate, where they could be found, and every step of their development, including molting. Her drawings highlighted the differences between males and females of different species as well, depicting butterflies from different angles to aid in identification. The book was popular with the public but ignored by other naturalists, because she had used common names rather than Latin descriptions.

SURINAME

When she was fifty-two, Maria became the first woman to travel independently to South America to study insects. In the country of Suriname, she observed and drew insects, reptiles, amphibians, and plants. When she returned home after three years, she published a book of illustrations based on her observations there. Many illustrators and naturalists were hugely influenced by her work and Carl Linnaeus (see Lab 2) used her drawings to identify more than a hundred new species, including a bird-eating spider, which was later named *Avicularia merianae* in her honor. Maria has several butterfly species named after her as well.

IN TODAY'S WORLD

Entomology is the modern name for the study of insects and how they relate to the environment and other living things. Insects can be both helpful and harmful. Understanding the life cycles of insects is essential to modern scientists studying everything from agriculture and medicine to solving crimes.

BIOLOGICAL ILLUSTRATION/ METAMORPHOSIS

Arthropods, such as insects, spiders, and centipedes and millipedes, are animals with jointed legs and skeletons outside of their bodies. Many arthropods live on plants. Like Maria Sibylla Merian, you can search for interesting insects and learn which plants they inhabit. Use a camera or do illustration by hand to document your discoveries.

MATERIALS

- Magnifying glass (optional)
- Camera or device with a camera
- Paper
- Watercolor paint, colored pencils, or markers

SAFETY TIPS AND HINTS

If you don't like to draw, print out the photographs of plants and insects and use them to document your discoveries.

PROTOCOL

1 Decide where and when you want to look for insects. Depending on where you live, it may be easier to find caterpillars in late summer. Patches of weeds where plants, such as milkweed, grow are often good places to look, but caterpillars can be found almost everywhere you see butterflies and moths.

Fig. 1. Look for insects on plants.

2 Research what plant species in your area play host to caterpillars. For example, monarch butterfly caterpillars can be found on several kinds of milkweed, and swallowtail butterflies often lay eggs on dill and parsley plants in gardens.

3 Go on an insect hunt. Look for caterpillars and butterfly eggs, and search for other flying insects and beetles as well. Use a magnifying glass to get a close-up view. *Fig. 1, Fig. 2.*

4 Take photographs of any bugs you find on plants, focusing on the insects, the leaves, and the entire plant. Take close-ups if you can. *Fig. 3, Fig. 4.*

5 Collect a leaf or two from the plants, if you think it would help you to draw them. *Fig. 5.*

6 Use a book, website, or app to help identify the insects and plants you found.

7 Draw and paint the insects you photographed. On the illustration, include their scientific names, and the date and location where you found them. Include close-ups of each insect and an image of the insect on the plant where you discovered it. If you found eggs, caterpillars, or other insects on a plant, include those in your drawing as well. *Fig. 6, Fig. 7.*

Fig. 2. Search for all kinds of insects, including beetles and other pollinators.

Fig. 3. Take photographs of insects on plants.

Fig. 4. Observe insect behavior.

Fig. 5. Pay special attention to plants where you find caterpillars. Collect a leaf or two to help you draw more accurately.

Fig. 6. Draw the insects you observed. Be sure to include the plants where you found them.

Fig. 7. Studying the photographs you took will help you make more accurate drawings.

CREATIVE ENRICHMENT

Search for a caterpillar or butterfly egg. Collect branches from the plant where you found the egg and put them in water. Replenish as needed to feed your caterpillar until it forms a chrysalis or cocoon. When it hatches, release the mature butterfly. Document the metamorphosis using your camera or paints. Identify and press any leaves you collected. (See Lab 15.)

THE BIOLOGY BEHIND THE FUN

Based on their research, scientists know that between eighty and ninety percent of all animals on Earth are insects. Most of these insects undergo what is known as complete metamorphosis.

Metamorphosis is the transformation from the immature form, such as a caterpillar, into the mature form, such as a butterfly. It takes place in two or more distinct steps. A butterfly, for example, goes from egg to caterpillar to chrysalis to winged creature.

Scientists believe that metamorphosis evolved over time, giving animals who undergo the process an advantage because the young aren't competing with the adults for food. For example, monarch butterflies, or *Danaus plexippus*, lay their eggs on milkweed. When the caterpillars hatch, they eat the leaves and often form their chrysalis on the same plant. Mature adult butterflies emerge from the chrysalis and use their hollow tongues to feed on nectar from any type of flower, leaving the foliage for more caterpillars to eat.

Carl Linnaeus (Carl von Linné) b. 1707

TAXONOMY/BINOMIAL NOMENCLATURE

A GARDEN

Carl Linnaeus loved plants from the time he was a small boy. Legend has it that when he was a baby, a flower blossom would instantly stop his crying. Carl's father was also interested in plants and gave Carl his own plot of land for a garden when he was only five years old. As he grew, Carl remained more interested in plants than he was in school and often skipped studying to go on plant-collecting expeditions.

A NEW SYSTEM

Because of his interest in botany, the study of plants, Carl's teachers suggested that he might enjoy medicine. He went to college to study medicine and botany, and while he was there he set up a new system for classifying plants. In 1732, when he was twenty-four years old, Carl went on a six-month expedition to Lapland to look for new plants and animals, and throughout his life he continued to go on these adventures.

THE PRINCE OF BOTANY

Carl Linnaeus became a medical doctor for several years to support his wife and children, but he continued to cultivate gardens and study new plants and animals. In 1753, he published a book called *Species Plantarum*, which organized and named all of the plants he'd encountered in his studies, and in 1758 he published *Systema Naturae*, which classified and named animals. These books were the official starting points for the way modern scientists name plants and animals.

TAXONOMY

Taxonomy is a system of classify things into groups. Linnaeus sorted living things using a naming system that moved from general categories to more specific ones. He divided organisms into either the plant or animal kingdom and then moved to progressively more specific levels, such as phylum, class, order, family, genus, and species. Since Carl's time, scientists have discovered new kingdoms of life and made new discoveries about how species are related.

BINOMIAL NOMENCLATURE

For his naming system, Linnaeus used two-part names based on the Latin language, which became known as binomial (two-part) nomenclature (naming). This was probably his most important contribution to science. The first part of a name in binomial nomenclature is generic, or general, and the second part is more specific. Each species is given a two-part name—for example, *Homo sapiens*—where the first part of the name is the genus (Homo) and the second part is the species (sapiens).

AN HONOR

In 1757, the king of Sweden granted Carl Linnaeus nobility for his achievements and his name was changed to Carl von Linn.

IN TODAY'S WORLD

Scientists today still use Linnaeus's binominal nomenclature to classify and name new species, using an expanded version with six kingdoms including fungi, eubacteria, and archaebacteria.

TAXONOMY/BINOMIAL NOMENCLATURE

Carl Linnaeus was a wizard of sorting living things into groups based on their physical traits. Try your hand at sorting animals into groups such as phylum, class, order, and family, then use what you've learned to play Twenty Questions.

MATERIALS

- Variety of plastic animals or photographs of animals cut from magazines (stuffed animals may be used as well).
- Friend or family member

SAFETY TIPS AND HINTS

If you're not familiar with the difference between mammals, birds, reptiles, amphibians, insects, and arachnids, look up the definitions of the words and list a few traits that will help you tell them apart. For example, mammals are warm-blooded and have live young. Birds have feathers and lay eggs.

PROTOCOL

1 Lay out animals and sort them into categories using a dichotomous key. *Fig. 1.*

2 To sort the animal *kingdom* into *phylums*, ask whether each animal is a vertebrate or invertebrate. Vertebrates are animals with their skeletons inside, such as humans and dogs. Invertebrates have skeletons on the outsides of their bodies. Insects and arthropods such as spiders and crabs, are invertebrates.

Fig.3. Use a dichotomous key to sort the animals into smaller groups.

3 Continue sorting animals by *class*. Do they have fur or no fur? Feathers or no feathers? Dry skin or moist skin? Soon, you will have them sorted into basic groups, such as mammals, birds, fish, reptiles, and amphibians. *Fig. 1, Fig. 2.*

4 Further sort the animals by *order*. Do they eat meat? Plants? Both? *Fig. 3.*

5 Sort them into *families*. Are they dog-like? Cat-like? Cow-like? *Fig. 4.*

6 To play Twenty Questions, have a friend or family member think of an animal they are familiar with. They shouldn't tell you what it is.

7 Make guesses to find out what animal they have chosen. Each guess must have a yes or no answer.

8 Begin by asking very general questions and go from there, depending on the answers. For example, start with questions such as "does it have fur?" or "is it a mammal." Depending on what you learn, your questions should get more specific, such as "is it a member of the cat family?" or "does it live in the salt water?" You will have twenty guesses to identify the mystery animal.

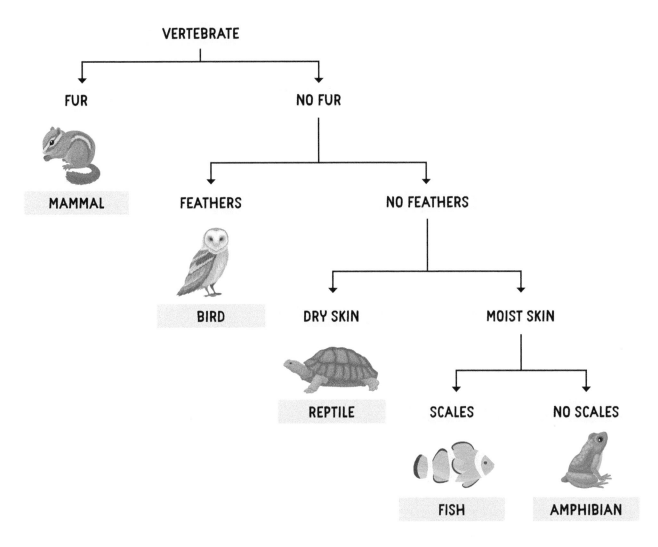

Fig. 1. A dichotomous key allows you to identify organisms based on a series of choices.

Fig. 2. Sort animals into groups using a dichotomous key.

Fig. 4. Sort the animals into families.

CREATIVE ENRICHMENT

Identify some plants and animals using binomial nomenclature, or make up and draw your own plant or animal!

Fig. 8. *Trifolium repens* (white clover)

Fig. 5. *Danaus plexippus* (monarch butterfly)

Fig. 6. *Tropaeolum majus* (nasturtium)

Fig. 7. *Melanoplus differentialus* (differential grasshopper)

THE BIOLOGY BEHIND THE FUN

Living things are separated into major ranks, moving from general descriptions to more specific ones: domain, kingdom, phylum, class, order, family, genus, and species. The game Twenty Questions sorts plants and animals into categories to identify a mystery species. Because the game gives you only two choices—yes or no—it mimics a scientific sorting tool called a dichotomous key. This game is played using common names, rather than scientific ones.

Linnaeus initially sorted things into one of three categories: plants, animals, and minerals. He categorized animals by the way they moved, and sorted plants into categories by their appearance. Since his time, our understanding of how life on Earth is related has grown enormously. We still use Linnaeus's binomial nomenclature (naming) system for genus and species, but today we have much more sophisticated techniques for identifying how living things are related.

The dogs we keep as pets look different because they are bred to select certain traits for size, fur color, and so on. Domestic (pet) dogs belong to the family *Canidae*, with the genus and species name *Canis familiaris*. The genus name is always capitalized the species name starts with a lowercase (small) letter.

Charles Darwin b. 1809
NATURAL SELECTION/EVOLUTION

THE ORIGIN OF DARWIN

Charles Darwin was born to a wealthy family in England in 1809. His mother died before he turned ten, and he was sent away to boarding school. When he was only sixteen, Charles went to medical school, but he soon discovered that he wasn't cut out for long lectures and gory surgeries.

AN EDUCATION

While in medical school, Charles also learned geology, marine biology, and plant classification. A freed slave named John Edmonstone, who had explored the South American rainforest with an English naturalist, taught Charles the art of taxidermy, which involves preserving animals by stuffing them. Eventually, Charles switched colleges, took up beetle-collecting, and graduated with a bachelor of arts degree.

A VOYAGE

In 1831, Charles joined an expedition to chart the shores of South America with captain Robert FitzRoy and his crew, aboard the ship HMS Beagle. His taxidermy skills came in handy as he collected specimens to send back to England for further study, and while exploring cliffs, he discovered the fossils of giant ground sloths. He was especially fascinated by the diversity of strange plants and animals he found on the Galápagos Islands, including giant tortoises that were different on each island.

A THEORY

When Charles returned home from his five-year voyage, he spoke with other scientists about what he'd found. The famous ornithologist John Gould told Charles that he'd discovered twelve new species of finches, which all looked similar but had beaks that ranged from tiny to huge. Darwin wondered whether the finches could have traveled from the mainland and changed over time, depending on what type of food they had available on each island. He bred pigeons to observe what changes he could create in their offspring. Charles also tested whether eggs and seeds could travel long distances in seawater.

SURVIVAL OF THE FITTEST

In 1859, Charles Darwin published a book titled, *On the Origin of Species*, which proposed a theory that life on Earth evolved over a very long period of time via a process that he called natural selection. His theory states that certain traits, such as longer or shorter beaks in finches, which allow species to survive in their environment are passed on to their young. The result of this phenomenon is that species change, or evolve, over time, adapting to their environment. His book presented evidence for the theory that all life arose from a common ancestor and branched off into diverse life forms best adapted to survive in their environments.

IN TODAY'S WORLD

Today, there is even more scientific evidence to support Darwin's theory of evolution by natural selection. Though he's most famous for his book *On the Origin of Species*, Charles Darwin also wrote a popular book about his voyage on the *Beagle*, figured out how coral atolls are formed, published a book on barnacles, and wrote a book about earthworms.

NATURAL SELECTION/EVOLUTION

In the Galápagos Islands, Charles Darwin discovered an astonishing array of species that had evolved to thrive in different environments. In this lab, create imaginary islands inhabited with birds whose beaks are best suited to their food supply. Then, replicate Charles Darwin's experiment to observe how eggs and seeds float on salt water.

MATERIALS

- Cardboard or paper
- Scissors
- Tall, clear container
- Markers or paint
- Sculpting clay
- Clear, wide container as least twice as tall as an egg
- Measuring cup
- Water
- Raw egg in shell
- Tablespoon
- Salt
- Stirring spoon
- Seeds such as seasoned seeds, vegetable seeds, or flower seeds

Fig. 1. Make islands with food supplies such as seeds, fish, or insects.

PROTOCOL

BEAK SHAPE PROJECT

1 Depending on the island where they lived, Darwin's finches had beak shapes suited for eating buds, insects, cacti, or leaves. Do an internet search for "bird beak shapes" and learn which shapes are suited for different foods.

2 Cut some "islands" out of cardboard. Use markers and clay to draw and sculpt a bird habitat. Put one type of food for each island, such as seeds, insects, flowers, or fish. *Fig. 1.*

3 Design birds for each island with beaks suited for whatever food supply you've placed on the island. For example, if you put insects on the island, the birds might have needle beaks. If you put nuts or seeds on the island, the birds would have cone-shaped beaks to crack them open. For flowers, they might have curved needle beaks, and birds who eat fish would have spear beaks. *Fig. 2, Fig. 3, Fig. 4.*

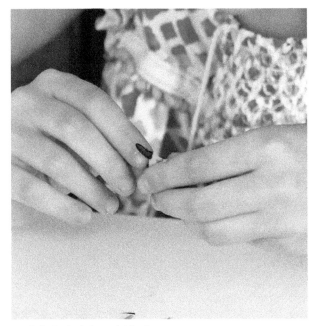

Fig. 2. Sculpt birds for each island.

Fig. 3. The birds' beaks should be suited to the food supply on the island they will inhabit.

Fig. 4. Make several islands.

CREATIVE ENRICHMENT

Research and recreate Darwin's finches from clay. Make an island for each finch type, including the food supply associated with each beak shape.

Fig. 1. Add a raw egg to a tall container filled with water.

Fig. 2. Add salt to the water.

Fig. 3. Continue adding salt until the egg floats near the top of the water.

Fig. 4. Add seeds, such as sesame seeds, to water.

OCEAN WATER EXPERIMENT

1 Fill a tall, clear container with water and place a raw egg in the water to see whether it sinks or floats in fresh water. *Fig. 1.*

2 Create water chemically similar to sea water by adding salt. To replicate sea water, add 2 tablespoons (35 g) of salt to 4 cups (1L) of water and gently stir until dissolved. *Fig. 2.*

3 Observe the egg to see whether it is floating.

4 If the egg isn't floating, add more salt, a tablespoon at a time. Keep track of how much salt you add. *Fig. 3.*

5 Add some seeds to the water to see whether they will float on salt water. *Fig. 4.*

6 Blow the egg and seeds from one side of the bowl to the other to see how wind could move plants and animals from one land mass to another. *Fig. 5.*

Fig. 5. Test whether seeds float and see whether you can blow them around in the water.

THE BIOLOGY BEHIND THE FUN

There are thirteen finch species which can be found today on the Galápagos Islands. The species all evolved from a single bird species called the grassquit, which arrived on the islands from South America. As they spread throughout the islands, each island's finch population adapted to the unique environment of their new home.

Galápagos finches are similar in shape, size, and color. It's difficult to tell them apart, but birds from each population have evolved certain traits which mark them as unique species and make it possible to identify them by habitat, beak shape and size, and by what they eat. The

Galápagos woodpecker finch (*Geospiza pallida*) employ sticks to pull insects out of trees, and the sharp-beaked ground finch (*Geospiza difficilis*) is called a vampire finch because it can use its sharp beak to drink the blood of large sea birds.

The buoyant (pushing) force of a liquid increases with density. For example, iron will float on mercury because mercury is denser. Eggs can float on salt water because the chlorine and sodium atoms in saltwater make it denser than fresh water.

John Snow b. 1813

EPIDEMIOLOGY/SOURCING AN OUTBREAK

DIRTY WATER

John Snow hated dirty water, but it made him famous. Born in 1813 and the oldest of nine children, he grew up near a sewage-polluted river in England, which flooded regularly. Once he grew up, he would only drink water purified by distillation.

MIASMIC VAPORS

In 1827, when he was only fourteen, Snow became a medical apprentice in a mining town where he witnessed the devastation caused by the deadly disease cholera. Cholera had been around for thousands of years, but at the time there was no cure and most people thought that diseases were caused by "bad" air, which they called miasmic vapors. Although scientists had observed microscopic organisms through magnification lenses, bacteria weren't yet associated with illness in humans.

ANESTHESIA

Eventually Snow went to medical school and studied to become a physician and surgeon. Surgeons were experimenting with anesthesia, which involved using chemicals to numb patients or put them to sleep during surgery. Snow became an expert on administering the chemicals, and Queen Victoria hired him to give her chloroform during the births of two of her children.

EPIDEMIC

When a cholera epidemic hit the West End of London in 1854, John Snow went to investigate. By talking to people in the affected area, he learned two things that convinced him the disease hadn't spread through the air. Several people who spent time with a victim sick with cholera were healthy, and several people who never interacted with a cholera patient had fallen ill with cholera. Back then, Londoners got drinking water from neighborhood wells. Snow made a map of the afflicted neighborhood, drawing dots where sick people lived. This now famous map led him to conclude that contaminated water from a well called the Broad Street Pump caused the cholera outbreak.

GERM THEORY

When the city removed the well's handle, so that no one could use it, the cholera epidemic in the neighborhood ended. After that Dr. Snow suggested public health measures such as handwashing and boiling water to prevent cholera, but few people took his advice. He died when he was only forty-five, but his work helped lay a foundation for the idea that germs in water and air cause disease. Just thirty years later, a scientist named Robert Koch (Lab 8) identified the bacteria that causes cholera and named it *Vibrio cholerae*.

IN TODAY'S WORLD

Today, epidemiologists like Dr. John Snow are more important than ever. Our global economy makes it easy for diseases to spread quickly, so it is essential to pinpoint the source of outbreaks and respond quickly in order to prevent pandemics.

EPIDEMIOLOGY/SOURCING AN OUTBREAK

John Snow was a famous disease detective who was well known for tracking down the source of a cholera outbreak caused by contaminated well-water. In this lab, you'll stage your own outbreak and identify the source of contamination.

MATERIALS

- ½ head (70 g) red cabbage
- 3-4 cups (705–940 ml) water
- Baking soda
- White (clear) vinegar (optional)
- 2 identical containers, such as drinking glasses, which will each hold 1 cup (235 ml) of liquid
- Baking sheet with a rim
- 25 small cups, drinking glasses or bowls (They do not have to be the same.)
- Teaspoon or eyedropper

SAFETY TIPS AND HINTS

Don't label the water and baking soda cups. The point of the exercise it to guess which is which!

PROTOCOL

1 Blend ½ head (70 g) red cabbage in 3 to 4 cups (705–940 ml) of water. Strain out cabbage and reserve purple juice. *Fig. 1.*

2 Add a little cabbage juice to each of two small cups. To one cup, add 1 teaspoon (5 g) of baking soda and stir. To the other cup, add enough vinegar to turn it bright pink. Cabbage juice is an acid base indicator and turns blue or green in a basic solution and pink in an acid. *Fig. 2.*

Fig. 8. Add a few tablespoons of cabbage juice to each cup or bowl.

3 For fun, place the cups on a baking sheet and pour the pink solution into the blue solution to perform a chemical reaction that makes carbon dioxide gas. *Fig. 3., Fig. 4.*

4 Add one cup (235 ml) of water to one of the two identical glasses. Add 1 tablespoon (15 g) of baking soda to the water and stir until dissolved. This cup represents a well containing water contaminated with a disease-causing microbe. *Fig. 5.*

5 Add 1 cup (235 ml) of water to the second container. This cup represents a well filled with clean water.

6 Arrange the 25 cups or bowls on the top of a table or counter as if they were houses in a neighborhood.

7 Have someone who is not playing detective put the two "wells" down in different parts of the "neighborhood," so whoever is playing disease detective doesn't know which well is contaminated. *Fig. 6.*

8 Use a spoon or eyedropper to give each "house" a few teaspoons of water from a nearby well. Give one or two "houses" water from the well across the neighborhood, but mostly add water from the nearest well. *Fig. 7.*

9 See who will get sick by adding a few tablespoons of red cabbage juice to each "house." *Fig. 8.*

(continued on page 30)

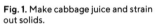

Fig. 1. Make cabbage juice and strain out solids.

Fig. 2. Add some baking soda to one cup of cabbage juice and vinegar to a second cup. Observe the color change.

Fig. 3. Pour the pink solution into the blue solution.

Fig. 4. The chemical reaction produces carbon dioxide gas.

Fig. 5. Add 1 tablespoon baking soda to a cup of water and stir until dissolved.

Fig. 6. Have someone place the two "wells" on opposite sides of the neighborhood.

Fig. 7. Use a spoon or eyedropper to give each "house" a few teaspoons of water from a nearby well.

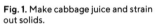

10 Look for a color change. Water from the contaminated well will turn the juice blue, while water from the safe well won't change the color much.

11 Solve the mystery of which well is contaminated. *Fig. 9.*

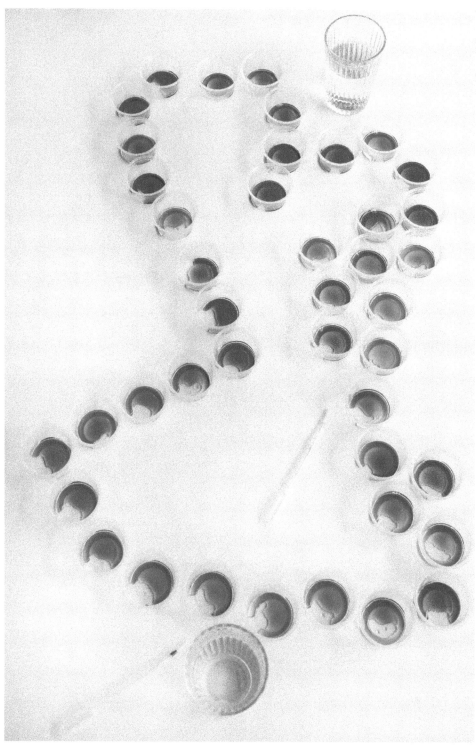

Fig. 9. Which well is contaminated with baking soda?

CREATIVE ENRICHMENT

Pretend that you're tracking down patient zero, the first documented case of a disease in an outbreak. Arrange fifteen cups, representing people, into three groups of five cups each. Put around 3 table-spoons (45 ml) of water in each cup. Have someone who is not playing detective remove the water from one container and replace it with 3 tablespoons (45 ml) of vinegar, so you don't know which container holds the vinegar. The vinegar represents an infectious microbe. Mix the liquid within the groups and between groups to represent human interactions. To test for "disease," add a few tablespoons of cabbage juice to each cup. Can you find the group containing patient zero? *Fig. 10, Fig. 11, Fig. 12.*

Fig. 10. After the vinegar-contaminated sample has been place in one group, mix samples.

Fig. 11. Add cabbage juice to test for infected individuals in groups.

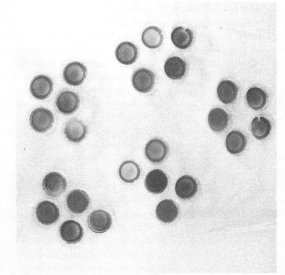

Fig. 12. Can you track down patient zero, or the group containing the original "infected" cup?

THE BIOLOGY BEHIND THE FUN

The world is full of microbes, including bacteria, viruses, and fungi. Most are harmless or even helpful to humans, but some, called pathogens, can make people sick. Diseases that can spread from one person to another are called contagious, or communicable diseases.

Many pathogens, such as the bacteria that cause cholera, can spread from humans to the environment and back to humans. They can survive in water, soil, air, and on sur-faces such as doorknobs. Many pathogens can also live in other animals, so it can be difficult to trace the origins of disease outbreaks.

Scientists such as John Snow who study outbreaks are called epidemiologists. Besides tracking down the patients who first got sick, they track the spread of disease, hunt down the natural habitats of pathogens, and analyze outbreaks to prevent them from happen-ing again.

⸗ LAB 5 ⸗

Gregor Mendel b. 1822

HEREDITY/POLLINATION

FARM KID

Gregor Mendel was born on a farm in Austria in 1822. When a teacher recognized his love of learning, Gregor's family worked extra hard so he could attend secondary school in a nearby city. Although he occasionally suffered from depression, Gregor excelled in physics and math. He graduated from the University of Olmtz in 1843.

A MONK

Gregor's parents expected him to return home and take over the family farm, but he had other plans. After studying to become a monk, he became a member of a religious community called the Augustinian Order. In 1851, he was sent to the University of Vienna to study the sciences and his botany professor taught him to use a microscope.

MENDEL'S GARDEN

In a monastery in the Czech Republic, Gregor Mendel began to study pea plants. He was interested in how living things passed observable characteristics called traits from parent to offspring. Peas were perfect research subjects because they grew quickly and it was possible to combine two plants to make "baby" plants. By opening the flower of one pea plant and dusting it with the pollen from another plant, he could study their offspring by growing the peas that resulted from the cross-pollination.

A DISCOVERY

Mendel's work with peas revealed that certain physical traits (features) were "dominant" over other traits. For example, when he crossed plants with purple and white flowers, their offspring had mostly purple flowers, so he called purple a dominant trait and white a "recessive" trait. These traits were passed from parent to offspring and certain traits, such as flower color, were independent of other traits, such as whether peas were smooth or wrinkled.

THE FOUNDER OF GENETICS

The passing of traits from one generation to another is known as heredity and Mendel published three "Laws of Heredity" based on his research on almost 30,000 pea plants. It wasn't until after Mendel's death in 1884 that scientists recognized the importance of his work. The invisible factors he studied, which give living things certain traits, are now called genes, and his experiments built the foundation for the modern science of genetics.

IN TODAY'S WORLD

Today, scientists understand more about the science of genes, but there is still much to learn. The DNA which makes up genes can be sequenced, giving researchers information that allows them to create medicines, vaccines, and treatments for several medical disorders. Plant genetics are used to help feed the world by producing crops resistant to drought and insects.

HEREDITY/POLLINATION

Gregor Mendel famously studied how traits are passed from one generation to the next by growing pea plants. Grow your own peas from seed and dissect their flowers or other flowers to learn how Mendel cross-pollinated plants.

MATERIALS

- Potting soil or dirt
- Pea seeds (two or more varieties)
- Garden or flowerpot
- Supports for peas, such as sticks, chicken wire, or lattice
- Small paintbrush
- Tweezers
- Magnifying glass

SAFETY TIPS AND HINTS

Follow the planting instructions on each pea seed packet for best results.

Fig. 3. Pick blossoms.

PROTOCOL

1 Observe pea seeds. *Fig. 1.* What traits (features) do you notice? Are they smooth or wrinkled? Big or small?

2 Plant peas in a garden or in flowerpots. Make a support of sticks or wire for the peas to climb as they grow. Are the plants tall or short? *Fig. 2.*

3 When the peas flower, pick a few of them. *Fig. 3.*

4 Study the blossoms under a magnifying glass. What color are they? *Fig. 4.*

5 Carefully pull open the closed part of the flower to find the stigma, which looks like a small stem inside the flower, and the anthers, which look like tiny threads tipped with pollen-covered beads.

6 Use tweezers to remove the anthers from a pea blossom. *Fig. 5.*

7 Open a second blossom and collect the pollen from the anthers on the tip of a paintbrush. *Fig. 6.*

8 To cross-pollinate the flowers, paint the pollen onto the stigma of the flower with the anthers removed. *Fig. 7.*

9 Now that you know how to cross-pollinate, try cross-pollinating the flowers from two different types of pea plants without removing the flowers from the plant. Collect the peas that grow from the flowers and observe them.

CREATIVE ENRICHMENT

Find the stigma and anthers in other types of flowers. Cross-pollinate two different varieties of edible peas or sweet peas and plant their offspring to study the resulting traits. *Fig. 8.*

Fig. 1. Observe pea seeds.

Fig. 2. Plant peas.

Fig. 4. Study the pea blossoms.

Fig. 5. Use tweezers to remove the anthers from a pea blossom.

Fig. 6. Collect pollen on a paintbrush

Fig. 7. Paint pollen on the stigma of another pea blossom

Fig. 8. Look for stigma and anthers on other flowers

THE BIOLOGY BEHIND THE FUN

Thanks to biology, and a concept known as "heredity," kids tend to look like their parents. In fact, the offspring of most plants, animals, and even bacteria show resemblance to their parents. Pea plants are no exception to the rule.

Inherited traits found in peas vary from plant height and flower color to the appearance of the peas themselves. Some pea seeds are smooth, while others are wrinkled. Mendel noticed that when he crossed two pea plants, such as tall one and a short one, he didn't get medium-sized plants. Instead he got all tall plants called "hybrids." When he crossed two tall hybrids, three out of the four offspring were tall, while the other one was short.

To figure out how pea plants were passing their traits onto their offspring, Mendel cross-pollinated pea plants again and again until he established basic rules about heredity, laying the foundation for the study of genetics.

Louis Pasteur b. 1822

SPONTANEOUS GENERATION/PASTEURIZATION

AN ARTIST AND A SCIENTIST

Louis Pasteur was born in 1822. He grew up in a picturesque French town called Dole which sits perched on a limestone ledge beside a large forest, overlooking the Doubs river. His father was a tanner who worked with leather, and they lived in a house near the canal. When he was young, Louis loved to sing, draw, and paint. An average student rather than a great one, Louis found he had a passion for science and earned degrees in chemistry and physics. He became a professor and married a woman named Marie Laurent. Sadly, three of their five children died of typhoid fever.

MIRROR IMAGES AND PASTEURIZATION

When Louis studied the acid crystals that form as grape juices turns into wine, he found two types of crystals, which were mirror images of one another. By separating the crystals into two piles under a microscope and shining light through them, he demonstrated that although mirror image molecules look almost identical, they behave differently. Other experiments conducted by Pasteur showed that by heating liquids such as wine, beer, and milk to a certain temperature, it was possible to kill harmful and unhelpful bacteria and yeast. This process, which came to be known as "pasteurization," kept consumers safer and made the beverages last longer and taste better.

SPONTANEOUS GENERATION

Louis Pasteur made extraordinary contributions to the field of microbiology as well. Using swan-necked flasks that trap airborne microbes, he disproved the popular theory of "spontaneous generation," which stated that living creatures commonly arose from sterile matter. Along with his contemporary Robert Koch, he developed the "germ theory" of disease, which states that microorganisms, such as bacteria, can cause disease in humans and animals.

VACCINATION

Variolation, an ancient method of making people immune to smallpox, involved dragging a thread dipped in smallpox scabs through a cut. The technique, which was often deadly, was improved in the 1790s by Edward Jenner, who developed a safer method of making people immune to bad cases of smallpox using scabs from cowpox (vaccinia virus).

While studying chicken cholera, Pasteur accidentally tried to infect his chickens with dead bacteria. When he realized his mistake, he reinfected them with healthy bacteria, but they didn't get sick with cholera. Louis realized that he'd created a new method of disease protection, which he named vaccination. In 1885, he developed a vaccine for rabies by injecting a boy bitten by a rabid dog with a compound of dried up tissue from a rabbit with rabies and saved the child's life. Pasteur worked on developing vaccines for several other diseases.

IN TODAY'S WORLD

Vaccines are still used every day, all around the world, to prevent deadly diseases.

SPONTANEOUS GENERATION/ PASTEURIZATION

To disprove the popular theory of "spontaneous generation," Louis Pasteur utilized a piece of glassware called a swan-necked flask. In this lab, you'll build a simple version of a swan-necked flask to re-create a simple version of Pasteur's original experiment and grow microbes from the air.

MATERIALS

- Two canning jars with screw-on metal lids with centers that can be removed.
- Plastic wrap
- Scissors
- Unopened bottle of clear apple juice
- Clean toothpicks or skewers
- Clean plastic bendable straws
- Clear tape (gift wrap tape)

SAFETY TIPS AND HINTS

- Juice should be clear and pasteurized, so microbial growth can be easily seen.

PROTOCOL

1 Run the jars and lids through the dishwasher or hand-wash them with hot, soapy water and rinse them well with more hot water just before doing the experiment. **Keep the jars upside down until you use them.**

2 Cut two 6 x 6-inch (15 x 15–cm) squares of plastic wrap large enough to easily cover the mouth of the jars.

Fig. 5. Use tape and plastic wrap to form a seal where the straw enters the jar. Trim off excess plastic wrap.

3 Open the bottle of apple juice and pour juice into the jar, so it is filled to around 2 inches (5 cm) from the top. Be careful not to breathe on the juice. *Fig. 1.*

4 Immediately place the plastic wrap over jar and screw the lid on.

5 Repeat with the second jar, so that each jar has a transparent covering.

6 Use a clean toothpick to pierce the center of each lid and carefully push a straw through, trying not to tear the plastic wrap. *Fig. 2, Fig. 3.*

7 Bend the neck of one of the straws, so it faces down at a 45-degree angle. Tape it into place as needed. Leave the other straw unbent. *Fig. 4.*

8 On each jar, use clear tape and plastic wrap to form a loose seal around the spot where the straw goes into the plastic. Trim off excess plastic. *Fig. 5.*

9 Make a hypothesis (guess) about which jar will have microbes growing in it first.

10 Allow the jars to sit at room temperature for a week or two, and observe what happens to the apple juice in the jar with a bent neck that keeps microbes out, and the one that lets microbes fall in. *Fig. 6.*

Fig. 1. Pour apple juice into freshly-washed jars.

Fig. 2. Use a toothpick or skewer to poke a hole in the plastic.

Fig. 3. Put a straw in each jar.

Fig. 4. Bend one of the straws so the end faces down. Tape it into position.

Fig. 6. Compare microbial growth in the two jars.

THE BIOLOGY BEHIND THE FUN

Bottled apple juice has been pasteurized (heated up) to kill any microbes that might be in the liquid. In this lab, dish soap and steam destroy most of the microbes inside of the jar, and the plastic wrap protects it from outside air.

The jar with the straight straw allows bacteria and fungi from the air to fall into the juice, where some of them can grow. The jar with the bent straw allows air in but keeps most microbes out. Chances are, yeast and bacteria floating in the air will get into the flask with the straight straw, causing the juice in that jar to become cloudy and spoil first, as microbes grow.

At a time when people still believed in "spontaneous generation" and thought that life could arise from sterile, non-living matter, Pasteur used an experiment like this one to prove there are invisible microbes everywhere, even in the air. These microbes, rather than spontaneous generation, were responsible for spoilage in food and liquids.

CREATIVE ENRICHMENT

This experiment may have helped Louis Pasteur come up with the idea of pasteurization, which involves heating liquids such as milk and juice to kill dangerous microbes, called pathogens.

Certain bacteria are good for us though, and we want them in our food, such as the lactobacillus acidophilus (Lack-toe-bassillus acid-off-oh-lus) in yogurt. Try making your own yogurt.

Carlos Juan Finlay b. 1833
BIOLOGICAL VECTORS/MOSQUITOES

WORLD TRAVELER

Juan Carlos Finlay y de Barrs, who later rearranged his name to Carlos Juan, was born in Cuba in 1833. Carlos attended school in France and England, but his studies were interrupted by illness twice, and he was forced to return home. Eventually, he traveled to the United States, where he studied medicine and graduated from Jefferson Medical College in Pennsylvania.

YELLOW FEVER

Upon returning to Cuba, Carlos became an ophthalmologist, married, and studied a dreadful disease called yellow fever. In addition to its namesake fever, the illness caused horrible muscle aches and could attack the liver, causing the skin of victims to take on a yellowish hue. Finlay hoped that if he could discover how the disease spread, he could save many lives.

A VECTOR

Carlos Finlay soon figured out that the disease was spread by mosquitos. They acted as "vectors" for yellow fever, carrying it from person to person. He even learned what type of mosquito carried the disease and suggested that controlling mosquitoes might stop the spread of yellow fever, but not everyone believed him.

MORE EVIDENCE

In 1900, the U.S. Army physician Walter Reed arrived in Cuba and Finlay told him about his theory that the mosquito species *Culex fasciatus*, which is now known as *Aedes aegypti*, carried the disease. Walter Reed conducted a set of dangerous, unethical experiments in which disease-carrying mosquitoes were allowed to bite human volunteers. The volunteers all got sick with yellow fever, proving that Finlay was correct.

A MONUMENTAL DISCOVERY

Once people started spraying for mosquitoes, yellow fever disappeared in Cuba and in Panama, where the United States was trying to build a canal. Controlling mosquitoes not only solved the problem of yellow fever, it helped to control another disease called malaria, which also spread by mosquitoes.

NO NOBEL PRIZE

Although Walter Reed always gave Carlos Finlay credit for discovering the vector of yellow fever, history credited Reed for "beating malaria." After his death in 1915, the Cuban government created the Finlay Institute for Investigations in Tropical Medicine in his honor. Finlay was nominated for a Nobel Prize in Medicine seven times but was never awarded the prestigious medal.

IN TODAY'S WORLD

Mosquitoes carry several disease-causing microbes, but they also play an important role in food chains. Scientists are still trying to learn how to control the number of disease-carrying mosquitoes without harming humans and other animals in the process.

BIOLOGICAL VECTORS/MOSQUITOES

Carlos Finlay learned from his research that the disease yellow fever is spread from person to person by mosquitoes. In this lab, you'll use water and coffee grounds to see how mosquitos can pass microbes from one person to another.

MATERIALS

- Several glass jars or clear drinking glasses
- Permanent marker
- Duct tape (optional)
- Water
- Red food coloring
- Coffee grounds
- Large syringe or an eyedropper

SAFETY TIPS AND HINTS

The coffee grounds should be fine enough to fit through the tip of the syringe.

Fig. 6. This project lets you see how mosquitos spread diseases such as yellow fever from one person to another.

PROTOCOL

1 If using jars, use a permanent marker to draw faces on the glass to represent people. *Fig. 1.*

2 Fill each glass with water and add a drop or two of food coloring so the water looks like blood. *Fig. 2.*

3 Add a spoonful of coffee grounds to one jar. The coffee grounds represent an infection-causing organism, such as flavivirus, which causes yellow fever. This jar now represents an individual with yellow fever. *Fig. 3.*

4 Move the jars around and clink them together. Like the coffee grounds in the glasses, the flavivirus that causes yellow fever can't move from person to person without help. The virus requires mosquitoes to transmit the virus from person to person.

5 The syringe or eyedropper will represent a mosquito, which is called the *vector* for yellow fever. Use a marker to draw mosquito-like features on the syringe, such as wings, eyes, and six legs.

6 Use the syringe or eyedropper to draw up some of the fake blood and coffee grounds from the "infected" jar. Move the syringe to another jar and inject the water in that jar with the coffee-ground contaminated water. This represents how mosquitoes pass viruses, bacteria, and parasites from one host to another. *Fig. 4.*

7 Take some of the blood from the jar you just contaminated and spread the disease from host to host until all the jars are "infected" with yellow fever. *Fig. 5, Fig. 6.*

Fig. 1. Draw faces on the jars or use duct tape to make faces on drinking glasses.

Fig. 2. Add red food coloring to water and mix.

Fig. 3. To one jar, add some coffee grounds.

Fig. 4. Use the mosquito-like syringe to draw up some fake blood from the jar "infected" with coffee grounds.

Fig. 5. Use the mosquito syringe to infect other jars with coffee grounds.

CREATIVE ENRICHMENT

Look up some other diseases spread by mosquitoes to learn how different microbes survive and multiply inside of mammals.

THE BIOLOGY BEHIND THE FUN

Biological vectors are living organisms, such as mosquitoes, that can spread disease from animals to humans, and from human to human through their saliva. The flavivirus that causes yellow fever is found in tropical and subtropical areas of South America and Africa.

Yellow fever is spread by the *Aedes aegypti* mosquito, which has distinctive white markings on its legs. This mosquito species is a vector for several other infectious diseases, including dengue fever, chikungunya, and Zika fever. Yellow fever victims often experience fever, aches, and pains, but the virus can attack the liver, causing jaundice, a condition that makes human skin look yellow.

Today, a single dose of a yellow fever vaccine prevents infection with the virus. The vaccine consists of a live, weakened form of the virus which primes the immune system to fight the virus without actually causing the disease. It has played an important role in preventing the spread of yellow fever from person to person.

Robert Koch b. 1843

KOCH'S POSTULATES/MICROBIAL FINGERPRINTS

MOUNTAINS OF SILVER

Robert Koch was born on December 11, 1843 in the mountains of Germany. His father was an engineer in the town of Clausthal, where silver and other precious metals had been mined since the Middle Ages. By the time he was five years old, Robert had taught himself to read, using the newspaper. In school, he was excellent at physics and math, but especially loved biology.

A NEW IDEA

When Robert was nineteen, he went to medical school. His anatomy professor Jacob Henle introduced him to the revolutionary idea that diseases were caused by living organisms too small to see without a microscope. After serving in the military during the Franco-Prussian war, Robert began doing research that would change the world forever.

ANTHRAX

At the time, a disease called anthrax plagued farm animals, such as cattle, sheep, and goats. Humans could also get sick and die from the disease. Working from a lab he had set up in his house, Robert Koch identified a rod-shaped bacterium in infected animals and demonstrated that it caused the dreaded disease. By infecting mice with anthrax bacteria, he also proved that bacteria-laden blood from animals sick with anthrax can infect other animals. It was the first time that anyone had ever linked a specific microorganism to one specific disease.

PETRI PLATES

To isolate pure cultures containing only one type of bacteria, Koch had to grow individual "colonies" arising from single cells. To grow colonies, Koch spread microbes on potatoes and shallow dishes filled with a jelly-like substance called gelatin. Eventually, he switched to using petri dishes filled with agar growth medium. (See Lab 10.)

KOCH'S POSTULATES

After that, Dr. Koch published a list of rules, called postulates, which could be used to prove which organisms caused certain diseases. His rules involved isolating one type of microbe from a diseased animal and using that same microbe to infect another animal. If he observed the same symptoms in that animal, he would then attempt to isolate the same microbe from the newly-infected animal. Using these rules, Koch discovered which microbes caused two diseases especially dangerous to humans: tuberculosis and cholera.

A NOBEL PRIZE

In 1906, Robert Koch was awarded the Nobel Prize in Physiology or Medicine. His work was the foundation for modern microbiology and infectious disease medicine.

IN TODAY'S WORLD

Today, scientists know more about microbiology and use modern technology, such as DNA sequencing, to help identify disease-causing organisms.

KOCH'S POSTULATES/MICROBIAL FINGERPRINTS

Robert Koch created a set of rules called postulates to help determine which microbes caused certain diseases. Like fingerprints, bacteria have unique features which allow identification. In this lab, play detective by comparing human fingerprints to see how unique features can help scientists identify disease-causing pathogens.

MATERIALS

- Paper
- Pencil
- Clear tape
- Magnifying glass
- Friend or family member
- Red pen or pencil

Fig. 6. Have a friend identify which of your fingerprint taped onto a drawing of a sick animal, by comparing to your fingerprints on the traced hand.

PROTOCOL

1 Trace one hand on a sheet of paper. *Fig. 1.*

2 Use the pencil to scribble on the paper, covering a small section with graphite. *Fig. 2.*

3 Rub a finger from the hand you traced in the graphite, so the skin of your fingertip pad is gray.

4 Put a piece of tape over the fingertip and lift your fingerprint. *Fig. 3.*

5 Tape the fingerprint down on the matching finger of the hand you traced. *Fig. 4.*

6 Repeat with each finger and your thumb.

7 Label your thumb and fingerprints with the numbers 1 through 5.

8 Each fingerprint on the hand you drew will represent a different disease-causing microbe. Like fingerprints, bacteria are unique. Robert Koch identified bacteria by studying their appearance under a microscope and using other chemical tests. Practice identifying the patterns in your fingerprints by studying them under a magnifying glass. *Fig. 5.*

9 Robert Koch looked for bacterial "fingerprints" in animals. Draw a mouse or rabbit on a clean piece of paper.

10 Have a friend or family member turn around. Choose one of your fingers to make a print from.

11 Tape the fingerprint on the drawing of the mouse. We will pretend that the fingerprint represents a specific bacterium that can make the mouse sick.

12 Color the eyes of the mouse or rabbit red to show that it is sick.

13 To identify the "bacteria" that made the mouse or rabbit sick, ask the friend or family member to use a magnifying glass to compare fingerprints and identify which of your prints matches the fingerprint in the mouse. *Fig. 6.*

Fig. 1. Trace one hand.

Fig. 2. Scribble the graphite from a pencil lead onto a piece of paper

Fig. 3. Rub a finger in the graphite and use a piece of tape to lift your fingerprint.

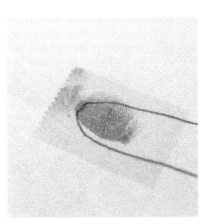

Fig. 4. Tape the fingerprint to the matching finger on the hand you traced.

Fig. 5. Practice identifying your fingerprints by pattern.

CREATIVE ENRICHMENT

Grow some microbes on agar plates (see Lab 10) and describe any characteristics of their appearance that might aid in their identification.

THE BIOLOGY BEHIND THE FUN

Pathogens are microscopic organisms that cause disease. They can be bacteria, viruses, fungi, or parasites. Bacteria are single-cell organisms which are significantly larger than viruses and can be seen under a microscope. Many bacterial species which infect humans will form colonies on agar growth medium (see Lab 10). Sometimes, bacteria can be identified by the appearance of their colonies on different types of growth medium.

Each pathogenic bacteria has its own "fingerprint" which can be used to help further identify it. By staining bacterial cells, scientists can sort them into two major categories, gram-positive or gram-negative, depending on how they absorb the dye. The gram-positive bacteria include streptococcal bacteria which can cause strep throat. Gram-negative bacteria include intestinal bacteria, such as *E. coli*.

After gram-staining, further tests can show how bacteria break down different chemicals. DNA analysis can also be used to test bacterial samples. Once a bacteria has been identified, it is easier for physicians to treat patients.

Ilya (Élie) Metchnikoff b. 1845

PHAGOCYTOSIS

RUSSIAN CHILDHOOD

The youngest of five children, Élie Metchnikoff was born in the village of Ivanovka in Russia in the spring of 1845. Élie's mother encouraged his interest in biology, and after finishing high school, which they called lycée, he went to Kharkiv University where he finished his degree in two years.

COMPARATIVE ANATOMY

Élie continued his education in Germany where he studied comparative anatomy by examining the body structures of different species of animals. His study of marine biology included many hours working with flatworms and cuttlefish.

INTRACELLULAR DIGESTION

While studying invertebrates, which are animals with no skeleton inside their bodies, Élie noticed something interesting. Certain cells in invertebrates, such as flatworms and starfish, appeared to eat foreign particles. He called this process "intracellular digestion."

STARFISH SCIENCE

Élie Metchnikoff learned even more about how organisms can fight infection by studying starfish larvae. When he put tiny thorns in them, special cells surrounded the thorns. From his research, he proposed that when a foreign body such as a thorn or a microorganism enters an animal, special cells surround and destroy the invading object.

A NEW OUTLOOK

Élie suffered from depression after his first wife died of tuberculosis and his second wife almost died of typhoid fever. However, scientists such as Louis Pasteur (Lab 6) and Robert Koch (Lab 8), among others, were learning what microorganisms caused these diseases. Advancements in science, along with his own exciting new discoveries, gave Metchnikoff hope. He continued his work with new energy, becoming the director of science at the Pasteur Institute in Paris, where he studied aging. He was the first scientist to suggest that certain microbes we have in our gut can affect our health, and recommend eating yogurt. Élie reportedly always wore the same hat, which he would accidentally sit on when he got excited about something.

IN TODAY'S WORLD

Élie Metchnikoff's won a Nobel Prize, along with Paul Ehrlich, for his important work on the study of immunology. Scientists today still study intracellular digestion, which they call phagocytosis, and are extremely interested in how intestinal microbes affect our health.

PHAGOCYTOSIS

Élie Metchnikoff spent count-less hours staring through a microscope to learn how phagocytic cells engulfed and destroyed foreign objects. In this lab, you'll make a large model of a phagocyte from cornstarch, water, and a balloon to get a hands-on experience with phagocytosis.

MATERIALS

- 1 cup (128 g) cornstarch
- ½ cup (120 ml) water
- Medium-sized bowl
- Paper cup or a container with a pouring spout
- Friend or family member
- White balloon
- Beads or other small objects

SAFETY TIPS AND HINTS

For kids with a latex allergy, a thick plastic bag could be used in place of a balloon.

PROTOCOL

1 Mix the cornstarch with the water to make a non-Newtonian fluid that acts like a solid when you move it around quickly and behaves like a liquid when it moves slowly. *Fig. 1, Fig. 2.*

2 Add some of the mixture to a paper cup or a container with a pouring spout.

3 Have a friend or family member hold the mouth of a balloon open and pour the cornstarch mixture into the balloon. *Fig. 3.*

Fig. 2. Play with the non-Newtonian fluid.

4 Tie the top of the balloon. The balloon represents a white blood cell.

5 Scatter small objects onto a surface to represent foreign objects in a body. Move your white blood cell balloon toward the objects and choose one to engulf. *Fig. 4.*

6 Put the small object onto the surface of the white blood cell and slowly push it toward the center of the balloon until the object completely disappears. This represents how white blood cells gobble up foreign objects, such as microbes, in your body. *Fig. 5, Fig. 6, Fig. 7.*

CREATIVE ENRICHMENT

Watch a video of white blood cells (phagocytes) engulfing and destroying bacteria.

Fig. 1. Mix cornstarch and water.

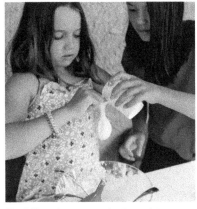

Fig. 3. Pour the cornstarch mixture into a balloon.

Fig. 4. The balloon filled with cornstarch solution represents a white blood cell.

Fig. 5. Push the object toward the center of the balloon.

Fig. 6. Use the balloon to surround and engulf a small object to see how white blood cells gobble up foreign objects.

Fig. 7. This project illustrates the process known as phagocytosis.

THE BIOLOGY BEHIND THE FUN

The word phagocytosis comes from the Latin words for "eat" and "cell." In phagocytosis, living cells called phagocytes engulf other cells or particles. White blood cells are one type of phagocyte, but free-living organisms such as amoebas and sponges feed using phagocytosis.

When white blood cells such as macrophages encounter a foreign body, they must first bind to it. Antibodies (see Lab 21) often help the phagocytes recognize foreign objects, such as bacteria. The membrane (outer layer) of the phagocyte moves around the foreign body until it is completely surrounded and inside a compartment called a phagosome.

Using harsh chemicals, the white blood cell then kills the bacteria, breaking down the foreign object. The compartment moves back to the outer membrane and fuses with it to release the fragments of the dead bacteria or foreign objects.

Fanny Hesse b. 1850
AGAR GROWTH MEDIUM

'LINA

Fanny Angelina Eilshemius's friends called her 'Lina. The oldest of ten children, she was born in New York in the summer of 1850 to wealthy Dutch immigrants. There were no vaccines to prevent childhood diseases back then, and five of her siblings died when they were very young. Growing up, she learned to cook from her mother and their servants. When she was fifteen years old, Fanny was sent off to boarding school in Switzerland to study French and economics.

A PARTNER

Fanny met her husband Walther Hesse when he was visiting New York during a stint as a surgeon for a German passenger ship. They met again when her family was in Europe and became engaged. She moved to Germany in 1874 to marry him and was first exposed to science in 1884 when Walther went to work in the lab of the famous microbiologist Robert Koch (Lab 8).

AN ARTIST

From a family of artists, Fanny proved herself to be talented at documenting Walther's research by making colorful medical illustrations of the bacteria he studied. To create accurate drawings of individual bacteria they saw under the microscope, and clumps of bacteria called colonies which could be seen with the naked eye, she had to learn about microbiology.

A LAB ASSISTANT

Besides educating and caring for their three sons, Fanny was Walther's lab assistant. She prepared food called culture medium for the bacteria they were studying. At that time, Robert Koch, Walther, and other microbiologists were having difficulty growing individual colonies of bacteria, which severely limited their research. They mixed nutrients with gelatin to make a flat, bouncy-like surface where colonies grew well, but on hot days the mixture melted. Certain types of bacteria also made chemicals called enzymes which could liquify the gelatin.

AGAR

Fanny Hesse had learned when she was young that a substance called agar-agar, or agar, made from red algae, could be added to jelly and pudding to make them resistant to melting. She had the idea to add agar to microbial culture medium and found that it created a long-lasting, heat- and enzyme-resistant surface for growing bacteria. Following her discovery, Robert Koch used Frannie's new agar culture medium recipe in his lab to grow bacteria and went on to make many great discoveries in microbiology. Sadly, Koch never gave Fanny or Walther Hesse credit for their contributions and they never profited from her brilliant idea.

IN TODAY'S WORLD

Agar growth medium is still used in labs around the world every day, in everything from molecular biology research to diagnosing strep throat in clinical labs.

AGAR GROWTH MEDIUM

Fanny Hesse came up with the idea of using agar to solidify nutrient plates for growing microbes, and scientists today still rely on her technique. In this lab, get a glimpse of some of the bacteria and fungi in your home or school environment by making agar media plates and swabbing surfaces to see what grows.

MATERIALS

- Water
- Clear plastic ware containers with lids, or petri dishes
- Agar (Can be found online and in most grocery stores.)
- Beef bouillon cubes or granules
- Sugar
- Plate or plastic wrap
- Cotton swabs

SAFETY TIPS AND HINTS

- Adult assistance or supervision is required for heating and pouring hot liquids.
- When working with agar plates, keep the lids on them whenever possible to avoid contamination by microorganisms in the air.
- Once microbes have grown, wash your hands thoroughly after handling the plates.

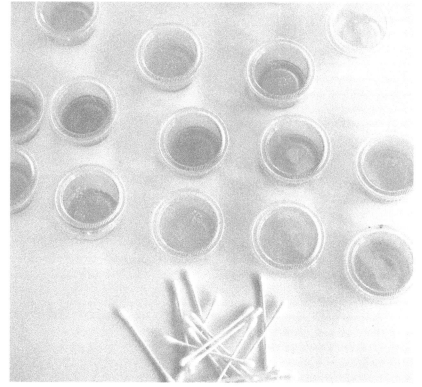

Fig. 3. Wait for the agar to solidify.

PROTOCOL

1 Make the microbial growth medium by mixing 1 cup (235 ml) of water, 1 tablespoon (5 g) of agar, 1 bouillon cube (or 1 teaspoon of granules), and 2 teaspoons (9 g) of sugar.

2 Bring the mixture to a boil on the stove or in the microwave, stirring at 1-minute intervals. Once the agar completely dissolves, remove the boiling liquid from the heat. Cover with a plate or plastic wrap and allow the mixture to cool for about 15 minutes.

3 Carefully pour the agar solution into clean containers, so it is around 1 to 1½ inches (2 to 3 cm) deep. Loosely place lids or plastic wrap over containers and allow them to cool completely. When the plates are solid, they're ready to use and can be stored in a refrigerator for a few days. *Fig. 1, Fig. 2.*

4 When the agar has solidified, label each agar plate with the date and names of the surfaces you want to test. You may divide each plate into 4 sections and label each section. Keep one plate unopened as a control plate. *Fig. 3.*

5 Rub a clean cotton swab around on the surface you want to test. Remove the lid and very gently rub or roll the cotton swab across the agar culture medium on a labeled plate. Test dusty surfaces, electronic devices, door-knobs, fingertips, or shake your hair over an open plate. *Fig. 4, Fig. 5, Fig. 6.*

(continued on page 29)

Fig. 1. Pour agar solution (growth medium) into clean containers

Fig. 2. Put lids or plastic loosely over containers immediately after adding growth medium.

Fig. 4. Use a cotton swab to sample microbes on surfaces.

Fig. 5. Swab a variety of surfaces.

Fig. 6. Gently transfer microbes from swab to agar growth medium.

THE BIOLOGY BEHIND THE FUN

Agar is a gelling agent made from red algae. Growing bacteria on solid agar growth medium helps scientists study microrganimsms and allows them to isolate pure cultures from a single colony. Agar plates stay solid at high temperatures and can't be liquified by bacteria.

Microbes live everywhere, from kitchen tables, deserts, and hot springs to human skin and intestines. Like zoo animals, each microbe has certain requirements for food, moisture, temperature, and oxygen. That explains why only a small percentage of the bacteria and fungi you picked up on your swab will grow on agar plates. Scientists use different recipes for making plates, depending on what microbes they're trying to grow.

The spots you see on your plates each arose from a single bacterial cell or fungal spore, which multiplied until millions of them formed a visible dot, called a colony. The size, color, and shape of colonies, along with chemistry and DNA analysis, helps scientists identify microbes growing on agar plates.

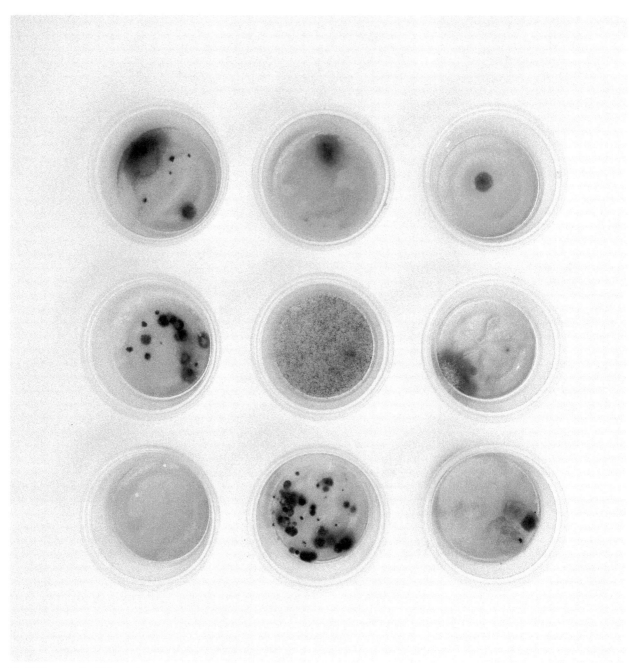

Fig. 7. Observe microbial growth.

6 When you're done collecting samples, set the plates on a flat surface with lids unsealed, but taped on. Flip them upside down to keep them from drying out.

7 After a few days, check the agar plates to look for growth. Tiny clear or white spots are probably colonies of bacteria, and larger, fuzzy spots are likely fungi. *Fig. 7.*

8 Record the shapes, sizes, and colors of the microbial colonies that grow on the plates. *Fig. 8.*

Fig. 8. How many different microbes do you see?

CREATIVE ENRICHMENT

Use a clean toothpick to lift one of the bacterial colonies from your plate and gently smear it onto a new plate in a zigzag pattern. Wash your hands, and let it grow for a few days. Are the bacteria that grow in the streak the same color as the original colony you picked? This is similar to a technique used by scientists, such as Robert Koch (Lab 8), to isolate pure bacterial cultures.

Santiago Ramón y Cajal b. 1852
NEURONS/NEURAL NETWORKS

OLD BONES

When Santiago Ramón y Cajal was eleven, he famously spent a few days in jail for destroying his neighbor's garden gate with a homemade cannon. Born in Northern Spain in 1852, he was an avid artist and gymnast who didn't like being told what to do. Santiago's rebellious personality got him kicked out of more than one school. When apprenticeships with a shoemaker and a barber didn't work out, his father, a professor of anatomy, took him to the graveyard hoping to convince his son to pursue a medical degree. His plan succeeded and Santiago, fascinated by drawing the bones they found, went to study medicine at the university.

INFECTIOUS DISEASE

After graduating from college, Santiago became a medical officer in the Spanish Army and traveled to Cuba, where he contracted the mosquito-borne disease malaria and was infected with tuberculosis. When he'd recovered, he returned to Spain where he went to graduate school, married, and had twelve children. Much of his early scientific research was spent looking through a microscope, focused on cellular structure, inflammation, and the bacterium *Vibrio cholerae*, which causes the disease cholera.

MEDICAL ILLUSTRATION

In 1887, Santiago and his family moved to Barcelona where he learned to stain tissue samples with special dyes that made certain cells and their structures easier to see under a microscope. He improved the staining methods and used them to dye brain and nerve cells, illustrating what he observed using the skills he'd developed when he was young.

CONES AND SPIKES

Santiago Cajal's drawings expanded scientific understanding of nerve cells and the neural networks they form to communicate with one another. He demonstrated that the nervous system was made up of individual cellular units which were later named neurons. He also described growth cones on nerve cells, discovered fingerlike dendritic spikes, and correctly guessed that nerve cells receive messages on one end and send them through their axons to the opposite end. A new type of cell he discovered and described was eventually named the "interstitial cell of Cajal."

A NOBEL PRIZE

In 1906, Santiago Ramón y Cajal and the Italian scientist Camillo Golgi were co-winners of the Nobel Prize for Biology in recognition of their work on the structure of the nervous system.

IN TODAY'S WORLD

Neurology, the study of nerves and the brain, continues to be an important field of research today, as scientists work to cure disease and understand how the human nervous system functions.

NEURONS/NEURAL NETWORKS

Santiago Ramón y Cajal correctly guessed that nerve cells receive messages and send them from one end to the other via the axon. Make your own collection of colorful neurons to see how signals travel across the axon, from one end to the other, allowing nerve cells to communicate.

MATERIALS

- Several chenille sticks (pipe cleaners)
- Beads
- Scissors
- Watercolor paint or pens and paper (optional)

PROTOCOL

1 Cut several chenille sticks into pieces 2 to 4 inches (5 to 10 cm) long. These will form the dendrites of the neuron. *Fig. 1, Fig. 2.* Lay one long, uncut chenille stick across another, around 2 inches (5 cm) from the top to form a cross. *Fig. 3.*

2 Twist the short piece of the cross down over the other pipe cleaner and twist it around itself to form a T shape. The vertical part of the T will represent the axon of the neuron. *Fig. 4.*

(continued on page 62)

Fig. 7. Thread a bead onto the long axon portion of the neuron to represent the electrical signal.

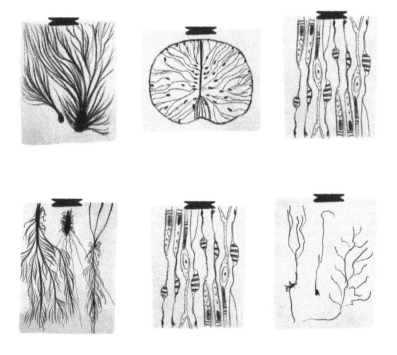

Fig. 1. Gather chenille sticks (pipe cleaners), beads, and scissors for this project.

Fig. 2. Cut some of the chenille sticks into pieces 5 to 10 cm long.

Fig. 3. Lay one uncut chenille stick across another one to form a cross shape.

Fig. 4. Twist the chenille stick down and around the long stem to form a T.

Fig. 5. Twist short pieces of chenille sticks around the arms of the T.

Fig. 6. Wrap the branches of the T to form a ball, representing the cell body of the neuron.

3 Twist several short chenille sticks around the top of the T to form branches. *Fig. 5.*

4 Wrap the top of the T around itself to form a ball, with the dendrite branches bristling out. The ball represents the cell body of the neuron. *Fig. 6.*

5 Twist a few more short chenille sticks onto the dendrites attached to the cell body.

6 Thread a bead onto the long axon portion of the neuron and twist the bottom into a small ball, or twist on another piece of chenille stick so the bead can't fall off. This end of the neuron represents the synaptic terminal. *Fig. 7* (page 60).

7 The bead represents an electrical signal. Position the bead near the cell body and dendrites and slide the bead across the axon to the synaptic terminal to see how a signal moves from one end of a nerve cell to the other. *Fig. 8.*

Fig. 8. Slide the bead from the dendrites to the synaptic terminal to see how electrical signals travel.

CREATIVE ENRICHMENT

Make several nerve cells and arrange them so synaptic terminals are near dendrites to create a neural network that demonstrates how signals travel from cell to cell. *Fig. 9.*

Find microscopic images of nerve cells stained using the Golgi technique (silver impregnation) and draw or paint them. Look up the artwork of Santiago Ramón y Cajal for inspiration.

Fig. 9. Make several model neurons and use them to see how nerve cells send signals to one another.

THE BIOLOGY BEHIND THE FUN

Thanks to a network of nerve cells, called neurons, when you touch something hot, you pull your hand away very quickly. These cells instantaneously carry the signal from your fingertips to your brain using electrical and chemical signals. Neurons can be very small or very long. Giraffes have neurons which are almost fifteen feet long, but they are so thin that they can only be seen under a microscope.

Branching dendrites on nerve cells carry information to the neuron's cell body, which transmits a signal to the axon. An electrical signal travels across the axon to the synaptic terminal, which then sends a chemical signal to nearby neurons. The chemical signal moves across a small gap to the dendrites of other neurons, which can pass it on to their neighbors.

To study nerve cells under a microscope, tissue must be stained using dyes that are absorbed into the cells. Santiago Ramón y Cajal used a technique called silver impregnation to study nerve cells. In his own words, the method made the cells appear "colored brownish black even to their finest branchlets, standing out with unsurpassable clarity upon a transparent yellow background." An improved version of the technique, also called the "Golgi Method," is still used by scientists today.

Charles Turner
b. 1867

BEES/ANIMAL BEHAVIOR

VALEDICTORIAN

Charles Turner was born in Cincinnati, Ohio in February of 1867, just over a year after slavery was abolished in the United States of America. His father was a custodian and his mother was a practical nurse. Charles excelled in school and was the valedictorian of his high school class. He continued his education at the University of Cincinnati, where he received an undergraduate and master's degree in science.

DISCRIMINATION

After teaching for a few years at Clark College, he went to graduate school at the University of Chicago, where he earned a Ph.D. in zoology and graduated with honors, becoming the first African American to earn a degree from that institution. Despite his advanced degree and the scientific papers he'd published, most major universities refused to hire black professors, so Dr. Turner went to work as a high school teacher in St. Louis, Missouri at a segregated school. He continued his research without funding or easy access to books and scientific journals, because African Americans weren't allowed regular entry into public libraries.

LEADING EXPERT IN INSECT BEHAVIOR

Even without a laboratory, Charles Turner went on to become a pioneer in the field of animal behavior. He designed mazes for ants and cockroaches and discovered that social insects such as ants and bees could learn to modify, or change, their behavior. Some of his most important research involved using colored disks and boxes to study the vision of honeybees and demonstrate that they could recognize shapes and patterns. Despite the obstacles he faced, Charles published more than seventy scientific papers in his career. He was a well-respected scientist in his field and was elected to the St. Louis Academy of Science in 1911.

CIVIL RIGHTS ADVOCATE

Dr. Turner was a leader in the St. Louis civil rights movement. He always believed that, like the creatures he studied, humans could change their behavior. Charles Turner hoped that through education, racism would one day end.

IN TODAY'S WORLD

Scientists today continue to study insect behavior, using everything from visual perception to swarming behavior, to enhance artificial intelligence systems.

BEES/ANIMAL BEHAVIOR

Charles Turner was a pioneer in studying animal behavior. Like the honeybees Dr. Turner studied, mason bees are important pollinators, but they rarely sting and don't have barbed stingers. This lab helps you build a home for mason bees.

MATERIALS

- Clear plastic bottle
- Scissors
- Twine, yarn, or heavy string
- Sculpting clay
- Paper straws
- Paper bag
- Pencil
- Tape

SAFETY TIPS AND HINTS

Younger kids should have an adult help cut the plastic bottle.

PROTOCOL

1 Use scissors to cut the bottom end off of a plastic bottle. If you have paper straws, cut the bottle so it is still slightly longer than the straws.

2 Run a piece of twine or string through the bottle so you can hang it up later. Tie it loosely to keep it out of the way. *Fig. 1.*

3 Add a little clay (if using) to one end of the straws to block them off. This step is optional, but mason bees like the closed tubes better. *Fig. 2.*

4 Put the straws in the bottle, clay end first so the open ends face out. *Fig. 3.*

Fig. 5. Inspect the mason bee house to ensure that the straws are tightly packed together and won't fall out.

5 To fill empty spaces in the mason bee house, cut strips of paper bag, roll them around a pencil and tape them to make tubes. Cut them to the correct length and add them to the bottle until the tubes and straws are packed tightly and won't fall out of the bottle. *Fig. 4, Fig. 5.*

6 Hang the mason bee house in a protected space away from where people are coming and going, such as on a fence or in a tree. Position it at an angle that will keep water out when it rains. *Fig. 6.*

7 Observe the mason bee house over several weeks and months, watching for bee activity.

CREATIVE ENRICHMENT

Recycle tin cans by filling them with straws to make mason bee homes. Paint the outsides of the cans with bright colors.

Fig. 1. Run a string through a bottle.

Fig. 2. Add clay to block one end of each straw.

Fig. 3. Put the straws into the bottle, closed-end first so the open ends face out.

Fig. 4. Make more straws from paper bags to fill empty space.

Fig. 6. Find a place to hang the bee house.

THE BIOLOGY BEHIND THE FUN

Mason bees are insects, classified as members of the genus Osmia, and there are around 300 species of them in the Northern Hemisphere. Unlike honeybees, which live in communities, mason bees are loners. They build their homes and nests in hollow twigs, cracks between stones, holes in wood, and even the occasional empty snail shell. They are called mason bees because they use mud to build their nests.

When a female bee is ready to nest, she collects pollen and nectar to pack into the narrow space she's chosen. After depositing the food, she lays an egg on a bed of pollen and seals the chamber with mud, before building a second chamber next to it until the space is filled with rooms for baby bees.

Remarkably, mason bees lay female eggs toward the back end of the space and male eggs toward the front because the males hatch first. Mason bees are important pollinators. They rarely sting and their stingers aren't barbed like those of some other bees.

Mary Agnes Chase b. 1869
AGROSTOLOGY/GRASSES

DAUGHTER OF A BLACKSMITH

In 1869, Mary Agnes Meara was born in Iroquois County in Illinois. Mary's father was a railroad blacksmith and her family changed their last name to Merrill to avoid the prejudice faced by working-class Irish immigrants. He died when she was only two years old and her family moved to Chicago. Mary's family was poor, so when she finished grade school, she had to go to work at the newspaper to support them and wasn't able to continue her formal education.

THE EXPOSITION

When she was only nineteen, Mary married a man in the newspaper business and changed her name to Mary Agnes Chase, but her husband died of tuberculosis a year later. In 1893, Mary and her nephew attended Chicago's Columbian Exposition, which was a huge fair, and saw an exhibit about plants. Mary was so fascinated by what she learned there that she decided to study botany.

A TALENTED ARTIST

Mary started her own field journals about plants and one of her professors was so impressed with her drawings that she was hired to illustrate books. She learned to use a microscope and worked as a meat inspector at the Chicago stockyards before returning to work with plants at the Chicago Field Museum. Eventually, she got a job with the United States Department of Agriculture, where she worked her way up from illustrator to lab assistant to principle scientist in charge of agrostology, the study of grasses. She traveled the world collecting more than 20,000 species of grasses and was the first to document several them.

A HUMAN RIGHTS ADVOCATE

Throughout her career, Mary Agnes Chase worked tirelessly to make science accessible and understandable to everyone. Sometimes, she risked her career to speak up for human rights. In addition to mentoring underprivileged students, including women who wanted to be botanists, she was a suffragist who was arrested twice, protesting for women's right to vote.

A COLLEGE DEGREE

In her long career, Mary Agnes Chase published more than seventy articles and books, including a popular guide to grasses for nonprofessionals, called *Agnes Chases's First Book of Grasses*, which is still in print. When she was eighty-nine years old, she finally received her first college degree, an honorary degree from the University of Illinois.

IN TODAY'S WORLD

The study of agrostology is still important today. Crop plants such as rice, corn, wheat, and sugarcane are all grasses. Healthy grasslands prevent soil erosion, and help with the problem of climate change by soaking up carbon dioxide from the air.

AGROSTOLOGY/GRASSES

Mary Agnes Chase traveled the world and collected over 20,000 species of grasses. If you can't go on a grass-collecting expedition of your own, try your hand at growing grass in clear plastic bags and flowerpots under different conditions to watch seeds germinate, and see what happens when grass grows in the dark.

MATERIALS

- Paper towels
- Water
- Small plastic zipper bags
- Grass seed such as lawn grass, wheat, oats, barley
- Permanent marker
- Masking tape
- Dirt or potting soil
- Small flowerpots or paper cups
- Clear glass container, such as a large glass jar to put over one pot (optional)

Fig. 3. Plant the same types of grass seeds in pots to see how they grow in dirt.

PROTOCOL

GERMINATION

1 Dampen a paper towel with water, fold it, and put it in a small zipper bag.

2 Add a few grass seeds to the bag on one side of the paper towel. Partially close the bag, but do not seal completely. Plant more than one type of grass, if you'd like to compare. *Fig. 1.*

3 Label the bag with a date and the type of seeds you planted.

4 Use tape to hang the bag in a window so you can see the seeds.

5 Check the seeds every day to observe germination. Watch for roots and a sprout to emerge. *Fig. 2.* Plant the same type of seeds in pots to compare how they grow. *Fig. 3, Fig. 4.*

Fig. 1. Plant grass seed in plastic bags on damp paper towels.

Fig. 2. Observe germination, watching for roots and a sprout to emerge.

Fig. 4. Compare growth rate and appearance in dirt to that in plastic bags.

Fig. 1. Grow grass under different conditions.

Fig. 2. Cover one container with glass or plastic

GROWTH CONDITIONS

1 Add dirt or potting soil to several small flowerpots or paper cups.

2 Plant the same type of grass in each pot by sprinkling grass seed on the dirt and then covering it with a thin layer of soil, or follow instructions on the seed packaging.

3 Label each container with growing conditions you choose, such as no sun, full sun, daily water, no water, and glass covering. *Fig. 1.*

4 Add a glass or plastic covering to one pot to create a greenhouse that traps heat and moisture. *Fig. 2.*

5 Allow grass to grow for several days, observing it daily for a week or two. When it is fully grown, compare the appearance of the grass which grew under different conditions. *Fig. 3.*

6 Place grass grown in the dark in a sunny spot to see how long it takes to turn green.

Fig. 3. Compare germination rate and appearance of grass grown under different conditions.

Fig. 4. Pull some grass up by the roots and study it.

Fig. 5. Find the nodules, or "knees," of the grass.

CREATIVE ENRICHMENT

Go outdoors and collect several grass-like plants, pulling them up from the roots, if possible. Cut the stems with scissors to identify whether they are grass, rushes, or sedges (see The Biology Behind the Fun, below). *Fig. 4*, *Fig. 5*.

THE BIOLOGY BEHIND THE FUN

Grasses use a chemical process called photosynthesis to turn sunlight, water, and carbon dioxide into energy so they can grow. Chlorophyll is a green pigment in plants which helps them absorb sunlight. Most plants growing in the dark don't make much chlorophyll.

If you see a grass-like plant, remember this rhyme: "Sedges have edges. Rushes are round. Grasses have knees that bend to the ground." Plants called sedges and rushes have solid stems and as the rhyme says, cutting a sedge reveals a triangular stem and cutting a rush stem will yield a round shape. The stems of grass are hollow, with joint-like solid nodes, which the rhyme calls "knees." The grass family, called Poaceae, contains around 780 genera and 12,000 species (see Lab 2). It is one of the most important plant families for humans, because we frequently consume grains from grasses, including wheat, rice, corn, and barley. Cattle eat an enormous amount of grass as well.

Susan La Flesche Picotte b. 1865

PUBLIC HEALTH/HOUSEFLIES

DAUGHTER OF A CHIEF

Susan La Flesche Picotte was born in June of 1865. She was the daughter of Joseph La Flesche, who had been made chief of the Omaha tribe of Nebraska in 1853. Following years of violence and displacement by European settlers, their people divided into those who followed the traditional ways and those, like her father, who believed that the only way to survive was to incorporate the ways of the white man.

She grew up in a log cabin with her three sisters and was sent to a boarding school on the reservation where indigenous students were forced to learn about European and American culture. By the time she went off to college, Susan was fluent in English and French as well as Omaha, which she spoke with her parents.

A LIFE-CHANGING EXPERIENCE

When Susan was eight years old, she watched an elderly woman on the reservation die in pain while waiting for a white doctor. They called the doctor four times, but he never arrived. Later, she recalled thinking, "It was only an Indian, and it did not matter (to him)." Perhaps this motivated her to eventually attend medical school at the Women's Medical College of Pennsylvania, the first medical school in the United States dedicated to educating women to be physicians. Susan took biology, chemistry, anatomy, and physiology classes, and she graduated as the valedictorian of her class.

HOMECOMING

Dr. Picotte returned home to Nebraska to find patients lining up at her door suffering from diseases that included tuberculosis and cholera. She worked twenty-hour days, traveling on miles by foot, horseback, or carriage to help people. After getting married and having two sons, she continued her work, which was unusual for a woman at that time. To control diseases on the reservation, she encouraged good hygiene (cleanliness to improve human health), including fresh air and screen doors to keep disease-carrying flies out of buildings.

"DR. SUSAN"

During her medical career, Susan La Flesche Picotte served more than 1,300 patients spread out over 450 square miles. She became known as "Dr. Susan" and became a local leader. Following the death of her husband, she worked as a defender of the ancestral land belonging to the Omaha tribe and raised enough money to build a hospital on the reservation. She died in 1915.

IN TODAY'S WORLD

Public health experts today understand much more about how disease is spread than they did in Susan La Flesche Picotte's time, but they are still working to find better ways to slow or stop the spread of diseases carried by flies and mosquitoes.

PUBLIC HEALTH/HOUSEFLIES

By encouraging both hand-washing and the installation of screen doors, Dr. Susan La Flesche Picotte taught her community about the importance of good hygiene in preventing the spread of disease. In this lab, you'll assemble a model of a housefly from sculpting clay, cotton swabs, and repurposed plastic to see how flies can spread disease from toilets and animal manure to food and other objects.

Fig. 3. Make wings for the fly.

MATERIALS

- Cotton swabs
- Sculpting clay
- Scissors
- Flat, thin, clear plastic from food packaging
- Permanent marker
- Paper
- Crayons or markers
- Stamp pad with washable ink

SAFETY TIPS AND HINTS

Use a stamp pad containing washable ink to make clean up easier.

PROTOCOL

1 Look up some photographs of common houseflies. *Fig. 1.*

2 Cut three cotton swabs in half to make six legs for a fly.

3 Use sculpting clay to create a fly approximately the right size to fit the legs.

4 Insert the swabs into the fly evenly, so it can stand on a flat surface. The cotton swab ends should form the feet. *Fig. 2.*

5 Cut plastic wings for the fly and use a marker to show the veins in the wings. *Fig. 3.*

6 On a piece of paper, draw several types of food. *Fig. 4.*

7 Pick your housefly up and fly it over to the stamp pad. The ink on the pad represents germs that might be on a piece of rotting food, animal feces, or a toilet. Have your fly land on the stamp pad to coat its feet with ink. *Fig. 5.*

8 Buzz your fly over to the food you drew and land it on your favorite dish. *Fig. 6.*

9 Observe how the "germs" transfer from the fly to your food.

10 Think about how a screen door in a house might protect food and other objects from germs carried by houseflies. *Fig. 7.*

Fig. 1. Look up images of houseflies.

Fig. 2. Sculpt a fly. Insert cut cotton swabs to represent legs and feet.

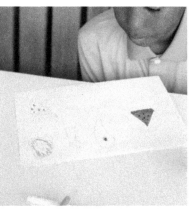

Fig. 4. Draw some food.

Fig. 5. Land the fly on an ink pad.

Fig. 6. Land the fly on your drawings of food to see how germs are transferred from the feet of houseflies onto food.

Fig. 7. Think about how a screen door on a house prevents flies from spreading disease.

CREATIVE ENRICHMENT

The mouthparts of flies pull food up using capillary action, a physical force that moves liquid through narrow spaces. Draw a dot on near the bottom of a strip of paper using washable marker. Place the bottom of the paper in water to see how water moves up through tiny spaces in the paper via capillary action.

THE BIOLOGY BEHIND THE FUN

Musca domestica is the scientific name for the domestic housefly. (See Lab 2 to learn about binomial nomenclature.) Houseflies have been spreading disease through human populations for thousands of years. They are even mentioned in ancient stories, such as Aesop's Fables.

Flies don't have mouths that can chew. Instead, their mouth parts have evolved to consume a liquid diet. The sponge-like retractable proboscis, which they use to eat, is covered in tiny grooves that pull food up using capillary action. They can taste food with special organs, called chemoreceptors, on their feet, which they frequently clean by rubbing their legs together.

Flies spit digestive juices onto food and feces where they land and their entire bodies are covered in bacteria. A recent study demonstrated that the pesky insects leave a trail of bacteria everywhere they land.

= LAB 15 =

Ynés Mexía b. 1870

PLANT COLLECTION/IDENTIFICATION

NATURE-LOVER

Ynés Enriquetta Juliette Mexía was born in 1870 in Washington D.C. Her father was a Mexican diplomat, and when her parents divorced, she moved to Texas with her mother. No matter where she was, whether it was Texas or Mexico, she loved taking long walks and studying the birds and plants she encountered. As a young woman, Ynés wasn't able to attend college, but even as an adult, she remained interested in the natural world.

CALIFORNIA

In 1909, Ynés moved to San Francisco, California. After experiencing personal tragedies, she was mentally and physically exhausted, but she found comfort in the beautiful mountains and redwood trees of Northern California. She became an active member the Sierra Club, which the naturalist John Muir had helped establish in 1892 to preserve Yosemite National Park, and she eventually took classes at the University of California–Berkeley.

SLEEPING UNDER THE STARS

Ynés was fifty-one when she started taking classes at Berkeley, and she went on her first major plant-collecting expeditions to in 1925, when she was fifty-five. Ignoring the male explorers who said that it would be impossible for a woman to travel alone in South America, she continued taking trips up and down the Americas, wearing pants, riding horses, and sleeping under the stars. She survived an earthquake, poisonous berries, and extremely difficult conditions on her quest to discover new species and document especially interesting plants, such as the wax palm tree, which could grow up to 200 feet (61 m) tall. Ynés Mexía joined other expeditions as well, including one to Brazil headed by Agnes Chase (Lab 12) and her colleague A. S. Hitchcock. Her assistant, Nina Floy Bracelin, prepared and helped identify the plants Ynés collected.

A SCIENCE COMMUNICATOR

Although Ynés Mexía was so busy collecting plants that she never finished her college degree, she gathered almost 150,000 species. In thirteen short years, Ynés discovered 500 new plant species and 2 new genera. Between expeditions, she gave lectures in San Francisco, sharing photographs of her journeys and teaching people about plants. Ynés suffered from prejudice because of her Mexican heritage, her age, and her gender, but everyone who knew her said that she was friendly, unassuming, and tough. She died in 1938 in Berkeley, California.

IN TODAY'S WORLD

Today, specimens collected by Ynés Mexía can be found in museums from New York to San Francisco.

PLANT COLLECTION/IDENTIFICATION

Ynés Mexía had a taste for adventure, braving earthquakes and poisonous berries to track down undiscovered plant species. You can get a taste of Mexía's passion for botany by gathering leaves and blossoms in your neighborhood or favorite park. This lab teaches you how to press and label plants to create an impressive collection of your own.

MATERIALS

- Scissors or pruning shears
- Paper bag
- Camera (optional)
- Heavy paper
- Newspaper
- Cardboard
- Heavy books or a plant press
- Glue

SAFETY TIPS AND HINTS

Before you go plant collecting, learn to identify harmful plants such as poison ivy, poison oak, and stinging nettles so you don't end up with an uncomfortable rash.

PROTOCOL

1 Go on a plant-collecting expedition in your neighborhood or in a park. *Fig. 1.*

2 When you find an interesting plant or tree, cut a branch, twig, or the entire plant, and put it in the bag to take with you.

3 If you have a camera, photograph the plant or tree you collected leaves from. Include extra photos, such as tree bark and stems, to aid in identification. *Fig. 2.*

Fig. 3. Lay the plants out.

4 Continue collecting plants and leaves until you have a nice collection.

5 When you return indoors, lay the plants out. Use a book, website, or app to identify what you've found. It is often helpful to look up plants commonly found in the general area where you collected them. The photographs should help, and leaf size, shape, and border are all features which will aid you in identifying what you've found. *Fig. 3.*

6 To press the plants, cut a sheet of heavy paper sized to each plant. *Fig. 4.*

7 Cut a piece of newspaper to the same size and lay it on the heavy paper. *Fig. 5.*

8 Place the plant leaves, stems, buds, and blossoms on the newspaper.

9 Lay another piece of newspaper on top of the plant and then add a second piece of heavy paper. *Fig. 6.*

10 Continue layering plants and paper until you have a small stack. If using a plant press, put it on either side of the stack and secure it. Otherwise, place the stack between two pieces of cardboard and add weight to the top to press the plants. Large, heavy books work well for pressing plants.

11 Wait several weeks before pulling the stack apart to see the dried plants. Carefully glue them to heavy paper and label them with their common and scientific names. Record the date and place where they were collected. *Fig. 7.*

Fig. 1. Go for a walk to look for plants. Bring a bag and some scissors or pruning shears.

Fig. 2. Collect and photograph what you find.

Fig. 4. Cut paper slightly longer than each plant.

Fig. 5. Cut a piece of newspaper to lay over the heavy paper.

Fig. 6. Sandwich the plants between newspaper and heavy paper.

Fig. 7. Label the plants when they are dry.

CREATIVE ENRICHMENT

Do some research to learn which insects inhabit the plants you collected. Try your hand at illustrating the plants and insects. (See Lab 1.)

THE BIOLOGY BEHIND THE FUN

Preserved plant specimens, such as those collected by Ynés Mexía, provide scientists with important information about plant diversity and distribution. Plants which have been dried correctly can last for hundreds of years. A collection of plant specimens and the recorded data about each plant is called a herbarium.

Plant "discovery" refers to the first time that a plant is recorded for science. Although we no longer have the plants, some of the first plant-collecting expeditions on record were undertaken by the Chinese and the Egyptians. In Victorian England, plant-hunting was a popular hobby and collectors would travel around the world to collect live plants for their gardens.

Today, scientists are also digitizing old plant collections and studying them to see how plant populations have changed through the years. Institutions, such as the Smithsonian National Museum of Natural History in the United States, now use DNA barcodes taken from living plants to identify species and store information.

Alexander Fleming b. 1881
FUNGI/PENICILLIN

A BIG FAMILY

Alexander Fleming was born in beautiful farm country at Lochfield near Darvel in Ayrshire, Scotland in 1881. After growing up surrounded by seven siblings, he went to college in London and then went to school for his medical degree. While he was there, Alexander became interested in microbiology after working with Sir Almroth Wright, who was a pioneer in vaccine therapy. On June 28, 1914, World War I began and Alexander found himself at one of the main hospital areas for wounded soldiers in Boulogne, France.

A DEADLY PROBLEM

In the hospitals, many soldiers who were saved by surgeons or didn't have life-threatening injuries died of infections. Alexander realized that the antiseptics being poured on wounds to kill bacteria weren't effective. They were only making the patients sicker and not reaching bacteria deep inside. He recommended keeping wounds clean and dry to kill bacteria, but few people listened to him.

AN ACCIDENTAL DISCOVERY

Following the war, Dr. Alexander Fleming continued studying bacteria, searching for substances in the human body that could kill harmful microbes. Legend has it that he discovered a substance he named "lysozyme," which could kill some types of bacteria, when his nose dripped into a bacterial culture. Another lab accident resulted in his discovery of penicillin. In 1928, he'd been on vacation with his family and came back home to a bunch of moldy petri dishes in his lab. "That's funny," he said, noticing that there was an area around one moldy spot where the bacteria had been destroyed. The bacteria-killing mold turned out to be *Penicillium*.

PENICILLIN

Molds are living organisms called fungi, which are not related to bacteria. Fleming named the bacteria-killing substance "mold juice" at first, and then changed the name to "penicillin," after the mold *Penicillium*. "One sometimes finds what one is not looking for," he said. In 1945, Alexander Fleming shared the Nobel Prize with Ernst Boris Chain and Sir Howard Walter Florey "for the discovery of penicillin and its curative effect in various infectious diseases." He died in 1955.

IN TODAY'S WORLD

Alexander Fleming later discovered that certain bacteria could develop resistance to penicillin. It is still used to fight infections today, but scientists are always searching for new antibiotics to treat strains of bacteria that are resistant to known antibiotics.

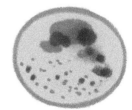

FUNGI/PENICILLIN

Alexander Fleming discovered the antibiotic called penicillin by accident, when some of his bacterial cultures were contaminated by blue-green mold, which we now call Penicillium mold. In this lab, see how many types of fungi you can grow on stale bread.

MATERIALS

- Slice of bread or several types of bread
- Clear plastic zipper bags
- Permanent marker
- Magnifying glass

SAFETY TIPS AND HINTS

Seal plastic bags as you study the molds, to prevent inhaling mold spores which can cause allergies.

Fig. 5. Look for blue and green *Penicillium* mold.

PROTOCOL

1 Cut bread into pieces small enough to place in a plastic zipper bag. *Fig. 1.*

2 Add several types of bread to different bags, if possible. *Fig. 2.*

3 Label the bags with the date and the bread ingredients, if you know what they are.

4 Put the bags in a dark, room-temperature drawer or a closet.

5 Keeping the bread in the bags, use a magnifying glass to check the bread every day for fungal growth. *Fig. 3.*

6 Record the color and texture of mold growing on the bread. Is it filamentous (like tiny threads), powdery, fuzzy, or slimy? *Fig. 4, Fig. 5.*

7 After you observe the mold, seal the bags and throw them away with the bread inside.

CREATIVE ENRICHMENT

Grow microbes on agar plates (Lab 10) and look for large, colorful fungal colonies growing beside the smaller bacterial colonies.

Fig. 1. Collect pieces of bread for growing mold.

Fig. 2. Add bread to bags.

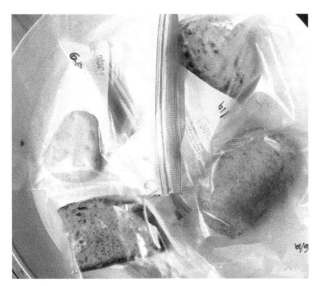

Fig. 3. Check bread for fungal growth.

Fig. 4. Record the color and texture of the fungal growth

THE BIOLOGY BEHIND THE FUN

Fungi are a kingdom of spore-producing organisms which feed on organic matter. They can be found all around the world, and the group includes molds, yeast, mushrooms, and toadstools. Fungi contain a molecule called chitin in their cell walls and do not perform photosynthesis.

Penicillium is a genus of the fungi family which contains more than 300 species. Besides being important for food production, some *Penicillium* species produce a chemical called penicillin, which can kill certain bacteria.

Some of the mold you observe growing on bread likely belongs to the *Penicillium* group. *Penicillium* mold are often green or blue and the shades can range from navy to turquoise. Some types of mold that grow on bread can make you sick, so it's best avoid eating moldy baked goods.

Ernest Everett Just b. 1883

CELL PHYSIOLOGY

THE DELTA

Ernest Everett Just was born in South Carolina in 1883 in Charleston, a city where the river meets the sea to form the largest river delta on the East Coast. When Ernest was only three years old, an earthquake almost destroyed the city, and when he was four, his father died.

Following his father's death, Ernest's mother moved their family to the countryside, where they were surrounded by the wildlife of the sea, the rivers, and the marshes. Whenever he got the chance, Ernest was outdoors exploring and observing nature. He learned to read in a school which his mother established. While his mother worked at the school, Ernest took care of his younger siblings. He survived an infection with deadly typhoid fever, which forced him to relearn how to read.

MOVING NORTH

After attending boarding school in South Carolina, Ernest moved north to New Hampshire to escape racial segregation and pursue his education. Besides working to pay his way through Dartmouth College, he had to support his brother and sister back home because his mother had died. After taking a biology class, he decided that he wanted to learn more about the cells which make up living things.

A PROFESSOR

All of Ernest's hard work paid off, and when he graduated from college, he became an English professor and then a biology professor at Howard University, where he also helped establish a college drama club. In the summers, he did marine biology research on the coast of Massachusetts, where he meticulously studied the eggs of sea creatures including sea urchins, sand dollars, and sand worms. He focused on cell physiology (how cells function) and carefully observed how the eggs changed during fertilization and development, publishing papers on his work in English and German.

DISCRIMINATION

Ernest's groundbreaking research made him famous around the world. Unfortunately, life in the United States wasn't easy for him. He was discriminated against because of the color of his skin and couldn't get the equipment he needed to do his work. Universities with mostly white professors refused to hire him. Eventually, he moved to France where he could independently pursue his research.

AN AUTHOR

Ernest Everett had a talent for explaining science in a way that was easy to understand. He wrote important books on methods of experimenting with the eggs of marine animals and on the biology of the surface of cells. Some of his most groundbreaking discoveries described how egg cells change when they contact a sperm cell, and how water moves in and out of cells.

IN TODAY'S WORLD

Ernest Everett's discoveries helped build a foundation for modern research into developmental biology, kidney disease, cancer, and in vitro fertilization.

CELL PHYSIOLOGY

Ernest Everett Just was interested in cell biology, including how water moves in and out of cells. In this lab you'll dissolve the shells of raw eggs in vinegar and soak them in corn syrup or water to make them swell or shrivel up.

MATERIALS

- Clear glass containers or jars
- Raw eggs
- Vinegar
- Corn syrup
- Water

SAFETY TIPS AND HINTS

Wash your hands after handling raw eggs. They can be contaminated with salmonella bacteria.

Fig. 6. The egg in corn syrup will float near the top until you push it down.

PROTOCOL

1 Put several raw eggs into a clear glass container, such as a bowl or jar. Add enough vinegar to the container to completely cover the eggs, and let them sit at room temperature for several hours. Notice the carbon dioxide bubbles that form as the calcium carbonate crystals in the shells react with the vinegar and dissolve. *Fig. 1.*

2 Put the eggs in the refrigerator overnight. The next day, they should feel soft and rubbery. If not, soak them longer. When the eggs are soft, rinse them in water and gently rub off any remaining shell until only the membrane remains. *Fig. 2.*

3 Hold an egg up to the light or shine a flashlight on it. Can you see the yolk? *Fig. 3, Fig. 4.*

4 Cover one dissolved-shell egg with water and let it sit overnight to see what happens.

5 Fill a second container with corn syrup and place a dissolved-shell egg in the syrup. The egg is made of mostly water. The corn syrup is a dense sugar solution so the egg will float near the top until you gently push it down. (See Lab 3 to learn more about density.) *Fig. 5, Fig. 6.*

6 Let the eggs sit overnight in the refrigerator.

7 Compare the eggs that sat in water overnight to the ones that sat in corn syrup. *Fig. 7.*

CREATIVE ENRICHMENT

Rinse off the corn syrup–soaked eggs and put them back in water overnight to see what happens. Add food coloring to test whether the chemicals in the dye can pass through the egg's membrane.

Fig. 1. Cover eggs in vinegar.

Fig. 2. Gently rub off any remaining shell.

Fig. 3. Study the egg inside the membrane.

Fig. 4. Shining a light on the egg will illuminate the yolk inside.

Fig. 5. Add one egg to a container of water and the other to corn syrup.

Fig. 7. Compare the eggs soaked in water to those soaked in corn syrup.

THE BIOLOGY BEHIND THE FUN

Chicken eggs are incubators for growing chicks. The egg white is made up of proteins and water, while the yolk contains nutrients for a growing chick and an ovum, or unfertilized egg cell. If the egg is fertilized, the ovum will divide into more cells and become an embryo.

Because developing chicks need oxygen, eggshells are full of thousands of microscopic holes called pores, which allows gases to move in and out of the shell. By dissolving the calcium carbonate crystals in shells to reveal the membrane underneath, it is possible to observe the process of osmosis.

Many cells in animals, plants, and bacteria use osmosis to move fluids in and out. Fluids containing large numbers of other molecules, such as sugar or salt, are called "concentrated" solutions. In osmosis, water moves across a membrane from a less concentrated solution to a more concentrated one. Corn syrup has a high sugar concentration. In this lab, you'll observe that water moves across the membrane, out of the egg, and into the corn syrup, making the egg shrivel up.

Jacques Monod b. 1910

GENE EXPRESSION

INFLUENCED BY DARWIN

Jacques Monod was born in Paris in 1910, but his family moved to the South of France when he was seven years old. Jacques' mother had been born in Milwaukee, Wisconsin. His father was a painter who was also very interested in science and read Charles Darwin's books (see Lab 3). He passed what he learned along to his son, sparking Jacques's interest in biology.

PARIS AND CALIFORNIA

When he was eighteen, Jacques moved back to Paris to pursue education at the university. He completed a science degree and a doctorate degree, studied in California, and worked at the Pasteur Institute and the famous Sorbonne University. In 1938, just before World War II, Jacques married an archeologist named Odette Bruhl and they had twin sons.

WORLD WAR II

Jacques's work, like that of many scientists around the world, was interrupted by World War II. During that war, many scientists had to join the military or flee their home countries to avoid being sent to concentration camps. When Jacques was awarded a Nobel Prize for biology in 1965, he spoke about returning to his lab in Nazi-occupied Paris during the war. "One day, almost exactly 25 years ago—it was at the beginning of the bleak winter of 1940—I entered André Lwoff's office at the Pasteur Institute. I wanted to discuss with him some of the rather surprising observations I had recently made. I was working then at the old Sorbonne, in an ancient laboratory that opened on a gallery full of stuffed monkeys. Demobilized in August in the Free Zone after the disaster of 1940, I had succeeded in locating my family living in the Northern Zone and had resumed my work with desperate eagerness."

THE LAC OPERON

Eventually, Jacques settled down as the director of the Pasteur Institute. Using bacteria, he assembled some of the first models for what we now call molecular biology. Jacques had been working for a long time to understand how the production of certain proteins, called enzymes, worked. When scientists discovered that DNA was a long chain that coded for different proteins, he finally had the key he needed to solve the puzzle. Dr. Monod showed that there was a kind of protein clamp that attached to DNA and kept other proteins from being made until they were needed. When the repressor got a signal, it unclamped from the DNA and new proteins and enzymes were made. The short segment of DNA he studied was named the lactose, or lac, operon.

IN TODAY'S WORLD

Jacques Monod's discoveries are the foundation of molecular biology. Every day scientists still use what he learned in their research on gene regulation.

GENE EXPRESSION

Jacques Monod was a pioneer in modern molecular biology. Although it's difficult to do molecular biology experiments outside of a laboratory, you can use snap-together blocks to represent DNA and learn how a process called gene expression can be regulated by proteins called repressors.

MATERIALS

Snap-together blocks

SAFETY TIPS AND HINTS

If you don't have a base for the snap-together blocks, use long blocks to make a base for your "DNA" model.

PROTOCOL

1 Look up an image of DNA. Study its structure. DNA contains codes for making proteins and codes that regulate how much of a protein is produced. In this lab, we will make a simple model of the lac operon, which regulates which proteins are made in bacteria when certain sugars are around.

2 Choose two long blocks and one short one of the same color to represent part of the DNA strand of the lac operon. Operons are units of DNA required for certain nearby DNA sequences, called genes, to be made into proteins. *Fig. 1.*

3 Choose a short block of a different color to represent a region of the DNA called the promoter. For the message in DNA to be made into proteins, a special protein called RNA polymerase has to bind tightly to the promoter.

Fig. 3. Add a block representing the repressor protein

4 Choose another small block of a third color to represent the operator region of the DNA. The operator region can bind to certain proteins to prevent the DNA from being made into RNA and then into proteins.

5 Snap the blocks together in order. *Fig. 2.*

6 Find a larger block of a fourth color to represent the repressor protein, which will cover both the operator and promoter. Add it to your model, spanning the operator and promoter. *Fig. 3.*

7 Choose another large block to act as RNA Polymerase. Note how you can't snap it onto the promoter when the repressor protein is there. No proteins can be made. *Fig. 3.*

8 Find some small white blocks to represent a sugar called lactose. Stick one of them to the repressor and pull the repressor off the operator. When lactose is available, it binds to the repressor and the repressor falls off the operator, allowing RNA polymerase to bind to the promotor region of the gene. *Fig. 4.*

9 Stick your RNA polymerase block to the promoter. Now, the genes that make up the operon can be transcribed (made into) RNA which can be translated into proteins that are used for the transport and metabolism of lactose. *Fig. 5, Fig. 6.*

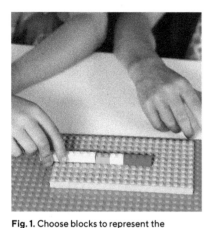

Fig. 1. Choose blocks to represent the lac operon.

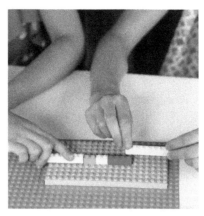

Fig. 2. Assemble the lac operon.

Fig. 4. Add blocks representing lactose to pull off the repressor.

Fig. 5. Stick the block representing RNA polymerase to the promoter block.

Fig. 6. RNA polymerase can now move down the gene to make RNA that can be translated into proteins for transporting and metabolizing lactose

CREATIVE ENRICHMENT

Search for illustrations of other genes and make models of them from snap-together blocks. Try to learn whether they are always turned on or are regulated, like the lac operon.

THE BIOLOGY BEHIND THE FUN

DNA is an information-containing material found in most in living things. Genes are sections of DNA that carry codes for proteins or other regulatory materials. When RNA polymerase attaches to the promoter of a gene, a strand of material called messenger RNA is formed using the DNA code. The messenger RNA is then translated into proteins, which serve essential functions in living things.

Monod showed that some genes, including the lac operon in *E. coli* bacteria, have clamps called repressors that attach to DNA near promoters and prevent other proteins from being made until they are needed. When the repressor gets a signal, it unclamps from the DNA and new proteins and enzymes are made.

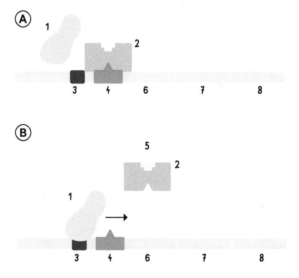

In Fig. A, RNA polymerase is blocked by the repressor. In Fig. B, lactose has unlocked the repressor and RNA polymerase can attach to the promoter to make messenger RNA.

LAB 19

Margaret S. Collins b. 1922
ZOOLOGY/TERMITES

AN EXPLORER

As a girl, Margaret Collins loved to explore in the woods near her house in West Virginia. Born in 1922, she was the fourth of five children. Her parents had both attended college, and her father had gone on to receive a master's degree. Her mother, who had wanted to be an archeologist, wasn't able to complete her undergraduate degree but she taught her children the importance of education, a lesson that Margaret never forgot.

CHILD PRODIGY

At the age of six, Margaret's advanced intellect was already evident. She was called a child prodigy, given a library card at the West Virginia State College Library and allowed to skip two grades. When she was only fourteen years old, Margaret graduated from high school and went to college. Graduating with a degree in biology, she also earned minors in physics and German.

STUCK IN THE LAB

Margaret completed her Ph.D. at the University of Chicago in the lab of Alfred E. Emerson, a termite expert. Not only was Emerson an expert, but he had the largest collection of termites in the world. Emerson was a good mentor, and shielded Margaret from some of the racism she faced. Unfortunately, like many male scientists at that time, he didn't want a woman doing field work with him, so while he chased down interesting termites, Margaret was stuck in the laboratory. Despite this, she managed write an important paper on termites.

A PROFESSOR

Zoology is the branch of biology that studies the animal kingdom. When she got her Ph.D., Dr. Collins became the first African American woman entomologist and the third female African American zoologist. She went to work as a professor at Howard University, but left because men and women weren't treated equally. She later worked for Florida A&M and spent a year at the University of Minnesota before returning to Howard University. During these years, she was fighting hard for civil rights.

GETTING INTO THE FIELD

By this time, Dr. Margaret Collins had come to think of herself as a field biologist and loved traveling the world to study termites in their natural habitat. In 1989, she discovered a new species of termite in Florida, called the Florida damp wood termite. She died in the Cayman Islands in 1996 at the age of seventy-three, doing what she loved best: studying termites.

IN TODAY'S WORLD

Scientist today still study termites, but not just because they can be destructive. Companies are attempting to duplicate termite saliva for industrial use, because it makes termite mounds so strong. Researchers are also interested in how the structure of termite mounds, which stay cool inside when it's hot outdoors.

ZOOLOGY/TERMITES

Margaret Collins knew that termite mounds, which are glued together by termite saliva, are incredibly strong. Modern chemists have concocted a synthetic version of termite spit which they hope to use for building stronger roads. It's fun to mix up some "termite saliva" at home from glue, cornstarch, and water. Use it to build termite mounds from coffee grounds.

MATERIALS

- Rimmed baking sheet
- Aluminum foil
- 1–2 cups of used, dried-out coffee grounds
- Water
- Washable school glue
- Cornstarch
- Sculpting clay

SAFETY TIPS AND HINTS

Save coffee grounds for this project ahead of time. Used coffee grounds can be quickly dried out in the oven on a baking sheet.

PROTOCOL

1 Line a baking sheet with foil.

2 Search for some images of termite mounds online.

3 Make "termite saliva" by mixing ¼ cup (60 ml) of water, ½ cup (120 ml) of washable glue and ¼ cup (32 g) of cornstarch. *Fig. 1.*

Fig. 5. Create a termite mound diorama.

4 Measure out ½ cup (64 g) dried coffee grounds and add them to a separate container.

5 Add 2 tablespoons (30 ml) termite saliva to the coffee grounds, mix them well, and form them into the shape of a termite mound on the foil-lined baking sheet. *Fig. 2.*

6 Repeat steps 4 and 5, but this time, add ¼ cup (60 ml) termite saliva to ½ cup (64 g) coffee grounds to build a second mound. *Fig. 3.*

7 Let the mounds dry and compare them. Which is stronger? Why? How will air flow through each of them? What else could you add to the termite saliva to build a stronger mound?

8 Look up images of termites and sculpt termites to add to the mounds. *Fig. 4.*

9 Make a diorama. *Fig. 5.*

Fig. 1. Make termite saliva.

Fig. 2. Mix termite saliva with coffee grounds.

Fig. 3. Form mixture into mounds and let them dry.

Fig. 4. Sculpt termites to add to the mounds.

CREATIVE ENRICHMENT

Develop a recipe for termite saliva that allows you to make the tallest, strongest mound possible. Adjust proportions of glue, cornstarch, and water, or try using other ingredients, such as nonwashable glue or cream of tartar. Determine the optimal amount of "termite saliva" to add to the coffee grounds.

THE BIOLOGY BEHIND THE FUN

Termites are phenomenal architects. Some species live inside the wood of trees and buildings, and others inhabit mounds made of clay, sand, soil, termite saliva, and dung. The above-ground part of a termite mound, called the "chimney," is porous, which means that it's full of tiny holes that air can travel through.

Honeycombed with tunnels, the chimney is a marvel of engineering which circulates air throughout the nest. While most of the termites live in nests at ground level, or below ground, their mounds are full of chambers where they store wood. In their nests, termites cultivate gardens of fungi, which helps them to digest the wood they eat.

Esther Lederberg b. 1922
LAMBDA PHAGE/REPLICA PLATING

THE GREAT DEPRESSION

Esther Miriam Zimmer was born in the Bronx of New York in 1922. She was seven years old when the Great Depression struck. Esther recalled being hungry as a child and often having just a piece of bread topped with juice squeezed from a tomato for lunch. She was very close to her grandfather, who taught her to speak Hebrew.

STRUGGLING SCIENTIST

When she was sixteen, Esther graduated from high school and won a scholarship to study at Hunter College, City University of New York. She loved literature, music, and French, but decided to study biochemistry. After college, she moved to California to pursue a master's degree in genetics at Stanford. To pay rent and buy food, she worked as a laboratory assistant and did laundry for her landlady.

MADISON, WISCONSIN

In 1946, Esther married a scientist named Joshua Lederberg and took his last name. They moved to Madison, Wisconsin where Joshua had been offered a job as a professor. Despite her master's degree and doctorate research at Stanford, Esther could only find work as Joshua's unpaid laboratory assistant. At the University of Wisconsin, she and Joshua did groundbreaking research on bacteria and in 1959 they returned to Stanford, where Joshua was made a tenured professor. Even with a Ph.D. and several major discoveries, Esther worked for fifteen years as a senior scientist before she was made an adjunct professor and was named the head of Stanford's Plasmid Reference Center.

A MAJOR DISCOVERY

Around 1950, as she finished her doctorate degree, Esther discovered that the E. coli bacteria she was studying had been infected by a type of virus called a bacteriophage. She named her discovery *lambda phage* and her research revealed that it was special because it could insert itself into the DNA of the host bacteria. While studying lambda phage, she also found a DNA sequence in bacteria that allows them to exchange DNA with other bacteria.

REPLICA PLATING

Dr. Esther Lederberg created an important laboratory technique called replica plating, which used a velvet stamp pad to transfer bacteria colonies from one plate to another in the exact same pattern. Using this method, scientists can easily find bacteria that have undergone spontaneous DNA mutations which allow them to grow on plates containing antibiotics.

IN TODAY'S WORLD

Lambda phage is an important tool for molecular biologists, and is used in research labs around the world every day.

LAMBDA PHAGE/REPLICA PLATING

Esther Lederberg was famous for discovering a virus called lambda phage, but she also invented an important laboratory technique called replica plating. In this lab, you can do a project simulating how replica plates are stamped, using potatoes and cotton swabs.

MATERIALS

- Potato
- Sharp knife
- Cotton swabs
- Toothpick or skewer
- Paper
- Paint
- Paintbrush

SAFETY TIPS AND HINTS

- Have an adult help slice the potatoes.
- If the potato slices aren't working well to stamp the patterns, stamp them directly onto paper. The idea of the project is to demonstrate that bacterial colonies can be picked up and replicated onto other plates.

PROTOCOL

1 Slice a potato into several round pieces around 1 inch (2.5 cm) thick.

2 Cut the tips off of cotton swabs so that only a very short piece of the stick is left.

3 Use a toothpick or skewer to poke holes in a random pattern in one of the potato slices. *Fig. 1.*

Fig. 5. Use a dry potato slice to pick up the paint from one of your model agar plates.

4 Insert cotton swab fragments into the holes to represent bacterial colonies growing on agar plates. (See Lab 10.) Try to make them all level, so they will stamp evenly. *Fig. 2.*

5 Repeat steps 2 through 4 to make a few more model agar plates. The pattern of colonies should be different on each plate. *Fig. 3.*

6 Trace potato slices onto paper to form several "plates" on the paper.

7 Paint the cotton swabs on each plate. *Fig. 4.*

8 Dry off the remaining potato slices. Use one of them as a pad to pick up paint from the painted cotton swabs on one of your plates. *Fig. 5.*

9 Stamp the paint onto another potato slice or onto the circles you drew on the paper to see how you could replicate the pattern on a new petri plate. *Fig. 6.*

10 If using potato slices to lift the pattern isn't working well, stamp the colonies directly onto the paper circles.

11 Repeat with the other plates.

Fig. 1. Poke holes in potato slices.

Fig. 2. Insert cotton swabs.

Fig. 3. Make several model petri plates.

Fig. 4. Paint the swabs.

Fig. 6. Make a replica plate by stamping the pattern onto another potato slice or onto paper.

CREATIVE ENRICHMENT

Grow yeast on an agar plate (Lab 10). Mix yeast and water together and use a clean toothpick to apply it to a plate in a pattern of dots. When the yeast has grown for a few days, use a jar with a paper towel or velvet over one end to try to stamp the yeast pattern onto a new agar media plate.

THE BIOLOGY BEHIND THE FUN

E. coli is a species of bacteria found in the lower digestive tracts of mammals, including humans. In research labs, these bacteria are essential tools for biotechnology. Not only are *E. coli* inexpensive to grow, but they divide rapidly. Scientists regularly use them for recombinant DNA technology because it is simple to add pieces of DNA from other organisms to *E.coli* and use the bacteria to produce foreign proteins.

When individual *E. coli* are spread on agar medium (see Lab 10), they divide quickly to form individual spots, called colonies, which are visible to the human eye. Each colony contains millions of genetically identical bacteria.

Dr. Esther Lederberg and her husband Joshua Lederberg used Esther's replica plating technique to show that DNA mutations (changes) occur frequently and randomly in *E. coli*. By stamping identical colonies from one agar plate to another, they were able to see that certain bacterial colonies had developed mutations that gave them antibiotic resistance whether they were grown on plates containing antibiotics or grown on antibiotic-free plates. This demonstrated that the DNA mutations were random and not caused by growth on antibiotics.

June Almeida b. 1930

CORONAVIRUSES/AGGLUTINATION

A NEW VIRUS

When June Almeida wrote a paper about a new kind of virus she'd discovered, scientists reviewing her paper told her that she'd made a mistake. June, who was one of the world's most skilled electron microscope technicians, would soon prove them wrong. She had, in fact, photographed and identified an entirely new kind of virus, which she and her colleagues later named coronavirus.

STRAIGHT TO WORK

Born in Scotland in 1930, June was a bright student, but she didn't have enough money to go to the university. When she was sixteen, she left school and went to work as a laboratory technician at a hospital, where she looked through a microscope for the first time. June proved extremely talented at histopathology, which involves studying slides of human tissue and identifying diseases.

ELECTRON MICROSCOPY

She eventually went to work in a lab in London, got married, and moved to Canada where she learned to use electron microscopes, which are powerful enough to magnify viruses. Although she didn't have a college degree, June quickly became so talented at microscopy that researchers she worked with made her a co-author on some important scientific papers about the structures of viruses.

CLUMPING VIRUSES

A British professor of virology named A.P. Waterson convinced June to return to England, where she was awarded a doctorate of science degree. Now called Dr. Almeida, June became the first person to visualize the rubella virus, which causes the German measles. She also pioneered a technique called *immune electron microscopy*, which uses antibodies to clump viral particles together so that they're easier to see.

A HALO

When a colleague sent her a sample of an unidentified virus to look at with her electron microscope, June thought it looked similar to the one she'd tried to publish a paper about before. This time people believed her when she said that she'd discovered an entirely new kind of virus. She and her colleagues named this new family of viruses coronaviruses, for the crown-like halo that was visible around the viral particles in June's photographs.

Later in her career, Dr. Almeida published important papers on a bird respiratory virus and the hepatitis B virus. She also came out of retirement in the 1980s to help take images of HIV, which causes the disease AIDS.

IN TODAY'S WORLD

Thanks to the work of June Almeida and her colleagues, scientists were recently able to identify the SARS virus and the SARS-CoV2 virus that causes COVID-19 as coronaviruses. What Dr. Almeida and her colleagues discovered about the structure of these and other viruses still helps scientists develop vaccines and drugs to keep humans and animals safe from them today.

CORONAVIRUSES/AGGLUTINATION

June Almeida pioneered a microscopic technique which used Y-shaped proteins called antibodies to make viruses clump together. In this lab, use sculpting clay and tooth-picks to make model viruses and antibodies to illustrate the clumping process called agglutination.

MATERIALS

- Sculpting clay
- Short wooden skewers or cotton swabs with the cotton cut off one end
- Toothpicks
- Tray or baking sheet

SAFETY TIPS AND HINTS

Small children should be supervised when using toothpicks and skewers.

PROTOCOL

1 Roll several pieces of sculpting clay into small balls and put each piece onto the sharp end of a skewer or on the stick end of a cut cotton swab. *Fig. 1.*

2 Stick two toothpicks into each sculpting clay ball to form a Y-shaped object. Each Y-shape you make represents an antibody. Antibodies are proteins made to recognize and bind to objects your body recognizes as foreign, such as bacteria, viruses, and fungi. *Fig. 2.*

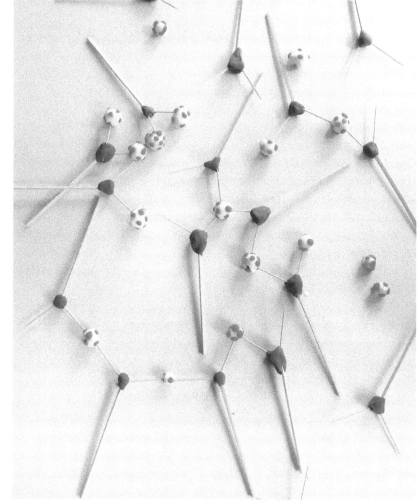

Fig. 6. Agglutinate the viral particles by attaching more than one antibody to some of the viral particles.

3 Create ten to twenty viral particles out of sculpting clay. Look up an image of the type of virus you want to represent and copy it as well as you can, or just make tiny balls covered in spikes to represent coronavirus. *Fig. 3.*

4 Lay the antibodies and viral particles out on a tray or baking sheet. *Fig. 4.*

5 Use the antibodies to capture the viral particles, attaching one virus at a time to a toothpick. *Fig. 5.*

6 To agglutinate the viruses, attach some toothpicks to the same viral particles. *Fig. 6.*

7 Neutralize the virus by attaching each particle to an antibody.

Fig. 1. Add sculpting clay balls to skewers.

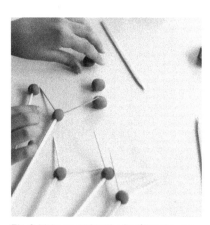

Fig. 2. Make several antibodies from skewers, toothpicks, and sculpting clay.

Fig. 3. Create viral particles from sculpting clay.

Fig. 4. Assemble 15 to 25 viral particles.

Fig. 5. Capture viral particles on antibodies

CREATIVE ENRICHMENT

Viruses come in many shapes and sizes. Look up information about viruses that cause common human illnesses, such as colds and influenza, to learn more about them, including how they spread and how vaccines are made.

THE BIOLOGY BEHIND THE FUN

Our bodies are constantly at war with microbial invaders. Certain viruses can hijack our cells to make millions of copies of themselves and make us sick. Proteins called antibodies are some of our body's best defenders against these invisible foes. Antibodies help the body kill foreign particles by tagging them for destruction by white blood cells. In addition, they make viral particles clump together, so they are not able to enter human cells. Scientists call the clumping of viral cells by antibodies "agglutination."

The parts of a foreign objects recognized by antibodies are called antigens. Antibodies are Y-shaped and the Fab (fragment antigen-binding) region on each arm is the part that binds to invaders, such as viruses. An antibody's stem is called the Fc (constant) region.

More than one antibody at a time can attach to a viral particle, and each antibody can attach to a different viral particle with each arm. This allows the antibodies to agglutinate the viral particles, making it easier for white blood cells to identify them, gobble them up and destroy them using a process called phagocytosis (see Lab 9). In most cases, large clumps of antibody-coated virus cannot enter cells to cause infection.

Luis Baptista b. 1941
ORNITHOLOGY/BIRD VOCALIZATIONS

TEA HOUSE FOR BIRDS

Luis Felipe Baptista, a famous ornithologist (bird scientist) of Portuguese-Chinese descent, was born in Hong Kong in 1941. When he was young, his father took him to a teahouse where people brought their caged birds so they could listen to birdsong while they drank tea. The experience ignited his passion for birds, and he started raising canaries of his own. As they grew, he sang to them and was surprised to discover that as adults, his pets sang exactly like he did.

SAN FRANCISCO

When he was a teenager, Luis's family emigrated from Hong Kong to San Francisco, where he got a job working as an assistant in the botany and ornithology departments at the California Academy of Sciences. He completed a bachelors and master's degree at the University of San Francisco and got a Ph.D. from the University of California–Berkeley, which was just across the bay.

THE SPARROW MAN OF GOLDEN GATE PARK

After graduate school, Luis moved to Germany to study the vocalizations (calls) of a bird called the common chaffinch. His research revealed that the finches had a language all their own. When he returned to California in 1975, he was interested in learning more about the song of another bird, the white-crowned sparrow. Eventually, he was able to recognize the voice of every white-crowned sparrow in San Francisco's Golden Gate Park and could recognize the difference between sparrow songs in locations all around the Bay Area.

A TEACHER AND A COLLEAGUE

The work of Luis Baptista helped scientists understand how birds learn songs and develop new ones. Dr. Baptista was a beloved professor whose students found him witty, funny, and charming. He worked with a diverse group of scientists and partnered with the San Francisco Zoo to reintroduce an almost-extinct species of doves into the wild. His book *The Life of Birds*, which he wrote with Joel C. Welty, inspired many students to study ornithology.

BIOMUSIC

Luis Baptista was famous for his ability to imitate sparrow songs perfectly, whistling them at half-speed. A lifelong music-lover, in one of his last lectures he talked about how humans incorporate bird song into their music and suggested that invention of music by birds and humans might be similar. Dr. Baptista died in 2000.

IN TODAY'S WORLD

Birds are found in ecosystems all around the planet. Today, scientists study the numbers, diversity, migration, breeding habits, and nesting grounds of birds to learn more about how our planet's environment is changing as the result of human activity.

ORNITHOLOGY/BIRD VOCALIZATIONS

Luis Baptista had an ear for bird calls and could recognize the voice of every white-crowned sparrow in San Francisco's Golden Gate Park. Try your hand at listening and whistling by going outdoors to watch and listen for birds. Can you learn to identify them by their vocalizations (calls)?

MATERIALS

- Bird identification book or app (optional)
- Notebook
- Pen or pencil
- Binoculars (optional)

SAFETY TIPS AND HINTS

- Apply sunscreen and insect repellent before setting out on your birdwatching expedition. For longer listening expeditions, pack a water bottle, snack, and a blanket or towel to sit on.
- Remember that identifying birds by call is difficult at first, but it becomes easier with practice.

PROTOCOL

1 Before you head outside, go online or use a book to research what species of birds are commonly found where you live. Remember that many birds migrate (move) from place to place, so depending on the month, you may find different species in your area.

2 Go to a website such as audubon.org to see what the birds in your area look like. Listen to recording of their calls. Use your notebook to write a description of the calls and songs.

Fig. 3. Close your eyes and listen for birds.

3 Go outdoors to a local park, field, or wooded area at a time when there won't be too many people around. Keep your eyes and ears open as you walk, watching for birds. If you see a bird, look for distinguishing features such as size, color, and markings. Binoculars are helpful for visual identification. *Fig. 1, Fig. 2.*

4 Stand or sit down in a quiet spot, close your eyes, and listen for birds. In addition to calls, you may hear wings or the drum-like sound of a woodpecker hammering on a tree. *Fig. 3.*

5 Try to isolate the call of a single bird. Record what you hear in your notebook. Is it a high or low sound? Is it a song or a short call? Does it match the descriptions you wrote down or the calls you listened to? *Fig. 4.*

6 Try to repeat the calls you learn by whistling. *Fig. 5, Fig. 6.*

7 Use a bird identification book or app to find the names of the species you see and hear. Record them in your notebook.

Fig. 1. Find a spot to look for birds.

Fig. 2. Binoculars are helpful for identifying birds.

Fig. 4. Try to isolate the call of a single bird.

Fig. 5. Repeat the bird call by whistling.

Fig. 6. Can you imitate their trills and whistles?

CREATIVE ENRICHMENT

Return to the same spot several times a week. Listen and watch for birds every day, recording what you discover in your notebook. Become familiar with the avian inhabitants of a park, field, or wooded area so you can identify the species that live there. If you return to the same area frequently, you may learn to identify individual birds by their call and appearance.

THE BIOLOGY BEHIND THE FUN

The best way to find birds is not with your eyes, but with your ears. Even experts in bird identification sometimes listen for the calls and songs of birds to distinguish species that look alike but have different vocalizations.

Birds make sound through a tiny organ called the syrinx. Some can only produce a few notes, while others have a wide vocal range for making trills and whistles. They use songs to attract mates and defend their territories and shorter, simple calls to talk to each other and warn of threats.

People who "bird by ear" use words such as trill, buzz, rich, thin, harsh, whistling, flute-like, bell-like, and metallic. Many birds are most active early in the morning and less active when it is very hot outside. It can be overwhelming to pick out the song of a single bird when many birds are singing, but with practice you should be able to identify the songs of the birds in your neighborhood.

Patricia Bath b. 1942
MEDICAL DEVICES/CATARACT SURGERY

A CHEMISTRY SET

Patricia Bath was born in the Harlem neighborhood of New York City in 1942. Her father was a subway train operator and her mother worked as a housekeeper when she wasn't taking care of Patricia and her brother, so she could save money for her children's education. Patricia's parents always encouraged her to work hard in school, and her mother sparked her interest in science when she bought Patricia her first chemistry set.

A SCIENCE-LOVER

Patricia was an outstanding math and science student in high school, and she discovered that she loved biology. When she was sixteen, cancer cell research she did at a workshop sponsored by the National Science Foundation was so impressive that it was included in an academic paper. After earning a B.A. in chemistry, she attended Howard University's College of Medicine, where she received her medical degree in 1967. Following the assassination of Martin Luther King Jr. that same year, she organized her fellow medical students to volunteer their time and talents to help people in their community who could not afford health care.

AN OPHTHALMOLOGIST

When Patricia Bath, now Dr. Bath, returned home to work at Harlem Hospital, she noticed there were more blind patients there than at a neighboring hospital where she also worked. She continued her education, doing a residency to become an ophthalmologist, which is an expert in eyes and vision. When Dr. Bath's research demonstrated that certain groups of people suffered from more eye problems than others, she wanted to understand why and help address the problem. She set up an eye clinic at Harlem Hospital Center, where they started doing eye surgeries. In 1972, Patricia got married and had a daughter named Eraka.

AN INVENTOR

After moving to Los Angeles, Dr. Bath continued working to improve surgical treatment for blind patients. She invented a medical device that dissolves cloudy lenses called cataracts, which can form on the eyes of older people. Once the cataracts are gone, new lenses can be put in. She patented four more devices for eye surgeries, and thanks to her inventions, people who were blind for decades were able to regain their eyesight. Throughout her career, Dr. Bath addressed issues in society that contributed to vision problems, such as poverty and inadequate access to health care. Dr. Patricia Bath was a partner of the American Institute of Blindness, whose motto is "Eyesight is a basic human right." She died in 2019.

IN TODAY'S WORLD

Dr. Bath's contributions to surgical equipment and eye care are still used in eye clinics around the world every day.

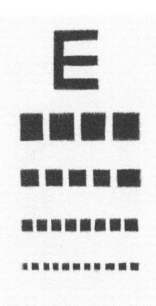

MEDICAL DEVICES/CATARACT SURGERY

Dr. Patricia Bath improved the lives of countless people with her inventions, such as medical devices for cataract surgery. Make binoculars with waxed paper lenses to experience for yourself how cataracts interfere with vision. See how replacing the cloudy lenses with a clear ones improves your sight.

MATERIALS

- Ruler
- Paper towel roll
- Scissors
- Waxed paper or parchment paper
- Clear plastic wrap
- Rubber bands

PROTOCOL

1 Use a ruler to measure the length of the paper towel tube. Use scissors to make a notch at the center of the tube and cut the tube into two cylinders of equal length.

2 Cut two pieces of waxed paper or parchment paper into squares that will easily cover the openings at the ends of the tubes. *Fig. 1, Fig. 2.*

3 Use rubber bands to attach the paper to the ends of the tubes and look through them as though you were looking through binoculars. How well can you see? *Fig. 3.*

Fig. 5. Look through the tubes again.

4 Remove the waxed paper coverings.

5 Cut two squares of clear plastic wrap and use rubber bands to attach them to the ends of the tubes as you did with the waxed paper. *Fig. 4.*

6 Look through the tubes again and note the difference in your vision. This is similar to how vision changes for the better when cataracts are removed and replaced with clear lenses. *Fig. 5, Fig. 6.*

CREATIVE ENRICHMENT

Think about other medical devices that have improved the quality of life for people or extended their lifespans. How many can you name? Do you know anyone who has had a hip replacement, a pacemaker, or cataract surgery?

Fig. 1. Cut out parchment paper covers for the tubes.

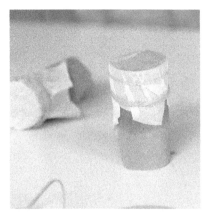

Fig. 2. Make one for each eye.

Fig. 3. Look through the parchment paper "cataracts."

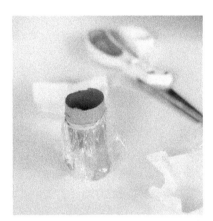

Fig. 4. Remove the waxed paper and replace it with clear plastic.

Fig. 5. Note the difference in your vision.

THE BIOLOGY BEHIND THE FUN

The lens in each of your eyes is suspended just behind the iris, which is the colorful part of your eye controlling the size of your pupil. Because it is a clear structure that focuses light onto the back of your eye to form images, a transparent lens is essential to good vision. Natural ocular (eye) lenses are made up of proteins and water.

The word cataract refers to the clouding of the lens. Cataracts usually occur in older people and form slowly, over time. People with cataracts often say they feel like they're looking through a dusty or frosted window.

Fortunately, Patricia Bath and other inventors pioneered techniques for removing natural lenses with cataracts and replacing them with clear, artificial lenses made of silicone or acrylics. Today, cataract surgery is very common and restores the vision of millions of people each year.

Danielle Lee b. 1974

PATTERN RECOGNITION/SCIENCE COMMUNICATION

LIGHTNING BUGS

Danielle N. Lee grew up in South Memphis, Tennessee. Her biological father is a musician and her other (step) father, who married her mom when she was eight years old, was a tractor-trailer tire repairman. Until she married, Danielle's mother worked for Memphis Parks Commission (the Parks and Recreation Department of the city) and raised Danielle with the help of her family in a big multigenerational household. Because of her mom's job, Danielle got to spend lots of time outdoors, exploring woods and fields. Looking for four-leaf clovers trained her eyes to see patterns, and she was good at it. She also loved collected lightning bugs and making garlands from dandelions and clover grass flowers.

LOOKING FOR PATTERNS

Even as a child, Danielle was fascinated by animal behavior. When flocks of birds moved across the sky, she studied the patterns in their movements and wondered whether their flight patterns were deliberate or whether they were trying to decide which bird to follow. She was never bored. During her free time, Danielle read books, listened to music, and did crafts. She enjoyed school and was good at it, but sometimes got in trouble for talking to her friends too much. Her teachers might have been surprised to discover that Danielle's excellent communication skills would come in handy later, when she became a professor.

A PROFESSOR

Danielle earned her bachelor's degree from Tennessee Technical University in 1996. At first, she wanted to go to veterinary school, but that didn't work out. Luckily, she started to study how small mammals called voles use their sense of smell and fell in love with the discipline of mammalogy. She got a master's degree from the University of Memphis and then a Ph.D. in biology from the University of Missouri–St. Louis. Today, Dr. Lee teaches mammalogy

(the study of mammals) and urban ecology at Southern Illinois University–Edwardsville. The focus of her current research is the behavior of African giant pouched rats, and she loves traveling to Tanzania to do field studies.

A SCIENCE COMMUNICATOR

Dr. Danielle N. Lee is well known for her ability to excite people about science. She does outreach to the public on social media, but she is especially passionate about her work as a role model and educator for underserved audiences. As a woman of color in science, she has faced extraordinary challenges and persevered. Dr. Lee has received many honors for her work, especially for encouraging minority participation in Science, Technology, Engineering, and Math (STEM) fields. She is a 2015 TED Fellow and a 2107 National Geographic Emerging Explorer.

THE FOUR-LEAF CLOVER

The logo for Dr. Lee's laboratory is the four-leaf clover. Each leaf is associated with a word: Behavior, Ecology, Justice, and Outreach. The study of science depends on observation, and the symbol reminds people who work with her that a multitude of perspectives are essential. She says that the clover represents why we need different perspectives: just as different patterns stand out to different individuals looking at the exact same field of clovers, a multitude of viewpoints bring the big picture into sharper focus.

IN TODAY'S WORLD

Research on mammals and animal behavior is essential to gaining insight into everything from economics to human health and wildlife conservation. Modern scientists, such as Dr. Lee, understand that it is essential to communicate with the public to gain support for research and to inspire future scientists.

PATTERN RECOGNITION/SCIENCE COMMUNICATION

As a child, Dr. Danielle Lee loved hunting for four-leafed clovers, which made her exceptionally good at observation and at recognizing patterns: two skills that contribute to her success as a biologist today. In this lab, you'll search for four-leafed clover to hone your pattern-recognition skills.

MATERIALS

- Small plastic bag
- Duct tape (optional)
- Newspaper and heavy books, or a plant press

SAFETY TIPS AND HINTS

Clovers with white flowers, which scientists call *Trifolium repens,* or "white clover" make it easier to find four-leaf clovers. A white stripe on their leaves forms a triangle when they have three leaves and more of a square, or butterfly, shape when they have four leaves.

PROTOCOL

1 If you don't know what clovers look like, find a picture of them online.

2 Go outside and search for patches of clovers in parks, lawns, or fields. *Fig. 1.*

3 Do a quick visual scan of the patch, to see whether anything jumps out at you. *Fig. 2.*

4 Hunt for four-leaf clovers until you find one or more. Be patient. It may take a while. *Fig. 3.*

Fig. 3. Keep hunting until you find a four-leaf clover. It may take a while.

5 Collect any four-leaf clovers you find and save them in a plastic bag. You can also stick them on a bracelet made of inside-out duct tape. *Fig. 4, Fig. 5.*

6 Collect a three-leaf clover and a blossom to add to your bag as well.

7 When you get home, press any clovers you found between two pieces of newspaper positioned between the pages of a heavy book or make a plant press. (See Lab 15.) *Fig. 6.*

CREATIVE ENRICHMENT

Add your clover to a plant collection. (See Lab 15.) Tell someone what you've learned about the science of clovers or practice your science communication skills by creating a short science video based on a science concept or experiment that interests you.

Fig. 1. Look for clovers.

Fig. 2. Do a quick visual scan.

Fig. 4. Collect clovers in a bag.

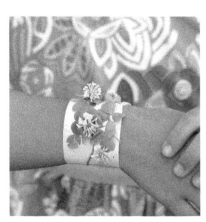

Fig. 5. Or make a clover bracelet.

Fig. 6. Press clovers to preserve them.

THE BIOLOGY BEHIND THE FUN

Clover, of the genus *Trifolium,* which means three leaves, is a member of the pea family. There are around 300 species of clover, and *Trifolium* can be found in almost every plant-friendly area of the world. Besides being important for agriculture and pollinators such as bees, clover plants have bacteria growing in their roots that add an important element called nitrogen to the soil.

Trifolium repens, also called "white clover," is very common. What most people call leaves on clovers are actually leaflets that make up a single leaf. Sometimes, the DNA in clovers undergoes mutations which allow them to grow an extra leaflet, which is often smaller than the other leaves. By crossing mutant clover plants, a Japanese man named Shigeo Obara was able to produce a 56-leaf clover which now holds the world record.

Some clover growers have reported that one in ten thousand clovers has four leaves. Based on that number and how many clovers can grow in a square meter, you would find a four-leaf clover once in every 1.2 square meters or 13 square feet of clovers.

Rae Wynn-Grant b. 1985

CARNIVORE ECOLOGY/ANIMAL BEHAVIOR

URBAN CHILDHOOD

Rae Wynn-Grant grew up in big cities. Born in San Francisco, she spent most of her childhood in California. Her mother is a writer and her father is an architect, so it surprised everyone when she decided to be a wildlife biologist. As a kid, she remembers being fascinated by television shows about wild animals, when she was a teenager, Rae dreamed about hosting her own nature show on *National Geographic*. In middle school and high school, she struggled with traditional tests and found math and science challenging, but Rae loved the things she was learning about the natural world and didn't allow less-than-perfect grades stand in her way.

ENVIRONMENTAL STUDIES

After high school, Rae attended Emory University where she learned about conservation biology, which focuses on protecting and restoring the diversity of life on Earth. She didn't get to see her first wild animal until she traveled to East Africa when she was nineteen years old. Rae studied for a master's degree in environmental studies from Yale University and then got a doctorate degree, studying how carnivores adapt (change) their behavior to adjust to landscapes altered by humans.

LIONS AND LEMURS AND BEARS

Rae loves bears. "They're just like people," she said in an interview with National Geographic Explorers at Work. "They just love to hang out." After finishing her Ph.D. in ecology and evolution from Columbia University, she did research called a post-doctoral for the American Museum of Natural History, studying the behavior and habitat of grizzly bears in Montana. Today, she studies bears in the mountains of Nevada and New York and does research on lions in Tanzania and lemurs in Madagascar. Dr. Wynn-Grant is interested in learning how animals, such as lions, change their movement and hunting patterns when humans live nearby. Her science work is dedicated to helping people and carnivores coexist peacefully all around the world.

A DREAM-COME-TRUE

Rae currently works as a large carnivore ecologist for the National Geographic Society and studies carnivore conservation around the world. She is a Visiting Scientist at the American Museum of Natural History and a professor at Columbia University and Johns Hopkins University. Dr. Wynn-Grant does some of her most important work as a science communicator, making environmental science accessible to broad and diverse audiences. Rae wants to show urban kids that they have a place doing work like hers. "Don't confuse performance with passion" is her motto. Dr. Rae Wynn-Grant is living proof that passion and hard work can make dreams come true.

IN TODAY'S WORLD

As Earth's population grows, people are moving into the habitat of wild animals. The work of Dr. Rae Wynn-Grant and other conservation ecologists is essential to the well-being of humans and animals who find themselves sharing space and resources.

CARNIVORE ECOLOGY/ANIMAL BEHAVIOR

Rae Wynn-Grant has spent many hours observing, tracking, and trapping wild animals to study their behavior. It's fun to observe animal behavior in your own neighborhood or a nearby park. In this lab, study insect behavior by trapping ants using cookie crumbs, and observe and record the behavior of larger animals, such as squirrels and birds.

MATERIALS

- Cookie crumbs
- Small plastic bag
- Rock
- Notebook
- Pencil or pen
- Magnifying glass (optional)
- Binoculars (optional)
- Camera (optional)

SAFETY TIPS AND HINTS

- Never try to pick up a wild animal. Keep your distance.
- To find ants quickly, place the ant trap in an area where you've seen ants before.
- If there are no wild animals nearby, study the behavior of pets, such as dogs, cats, and fish.

PROTOCOL

ANT TRAP

1 Put a few cookie crumbs inside a plastic bag. *Fig. 1.*

2 Find an outdoor location away from foot and car traffic. Place the bag on the ground.

Fig. 4. You may be surprised at what you discover lying on the ground.

3 Make sure that the bag is not sealed tightly, so that ants can crawl inside to the crumbs. Place a rock on the bag so it won't blow away.

4 Check the bag every few hours or the next day to look for ants. If you don't see any after a day or two, move the bag to a new location.

5 Observe the behavior of the ants and record it in your notebook. Date your observations and describe the size, color, and any other features that might help you identify the ants. Use a magnifying glass to look closely. *Fig. 2.*

ANIMAL OBSERVATION

1 Look for wild creatures in your neighborhood such as birds, squirrels, and rabbits. Observe them out a window or go for a walk to look for animals and signs of wild animals, such as footprints, scat (manure), holes, and nests. *Fig. 3, Fig. 4.*

2 Use a notebook and a camera to record what you find, including the date and time you see animals.

3 Take notes on what you observe the animals doing. Are they eating? What are they eating? How to they interact with their environment and other animals? *Fig. 5.*

4 Describe how the animals look. Use binoculars for a closer look. Are they healthy? Note any characteristic markings or features that might help you recognize them if you saw them again. *Fig. 6.*

Fig. 1. Place cookie crumbs in a clear bag.

Fig. 2. Study the ants you trap.

Fig. 3. Look for signs of wild animals.

Fig. 5. Observe arthropods such as insects, too.

Fig. 6. Use binoculars for a closer look.

Fig. 7. Observe animals with a friend and compare notes.

5 Think about how human behavior might affect the habitat (homes), food supply, and behavior of the animals you see.

6 Watch for animals at the same spot several times. Do they appear regularly? What time of day are you most likely to see them? *Fig. 7.*

CREATIVE ENRICHMENT

Use a camera to photograph the wildlife you discover. Photographs can help you get a closer look at individual animals and aid in the identification of different species.

THE BIOLOGY BEHIND THE FUN

Studying animal behavior requires patience. Often it takes time to locate animals, and once researchers find them, their behavior must be observed over a long period of time. The famous primatologist Jane Goodall regularly spent hours, days, or even weeks sitting around, waiting for the chimpanzees she studied to come into view.

Whether observing birds, squirrels, or bears, scientists understand the importance of keeping enough distance between the observer and the wild animal. This is important for safety when studying certain animals. In addition, the presence of a human will cause most wild animals to change their behavior.

Modern technology has made it possible to attach tags to animals which allows scientists to track their movement from afar. Radio signal transmitters on collars can be attached to large carnivores such as lions and smaller ones, such as horned lizards. Tracking wild animals allows researchers to understand how they behave in the wild and how their movement changes as a result of human activity.

GLOSSARY

Agar Growth Medium: A stable, sterile substance containing nutrients that allows the growth and isolation of individual colonies of microorganisms

Agglutination: The clumping of bacteria, viral particles, or cells in the presence of large, Y-shaped proteins called antibodies

Arthropod: An animal with no backbone or internal skeleton (invertebrate), such as lobsters, spiders, beetles, butterflies, and mites

Binomial Nomenclature: A two-term system for naming species of living organism, such as a plant or animal. The first name indicates the genus and the second tells you the species.

Biology: The study of life and living organisms. There are many subfields including: botany (plants) and related specialties such as agrostology (grasses); ecology (organisms and their environments); entomology (insects); epidemiology (disease in populations); genetics (heredity and variation); microbiology (microscopic organisms such as bacteria, viruses, and fungi); medical specialties, such as ophthalmology (eyes); ornithology (birds); physiology (biological functions); taxonomy (scientific classification); and zoology (animals).

Dichotomous Key: A method of classification based on a series of choices

Diversity: The variety of different living organisms in an ecosystem

DNA: Deoxyribonucleic acid: A chain-like molecule found in living organisms and some viruses. DNA looks like a twisted ladder and carries a sequence of genetic information necessary for reproduction, development, growth, and function.

Electron Microscope: An instrument which uses a beam of negatively charged particles called electrons instead of light to create a large view of extremely small objects

Evolution: A process of gradual change and diversification of species across many generations

Fungi: A classification of organisms, such as molds, mildews, mushrooms, and yeasts

Gene Expression: A process in which information encoded on a gene is copied from DNA (deoxyribonucleic acid) into messenger RNA (ribonucleic acid) and translated into a protein

Immune: Having biological protection or resistance to a certain disease after having been vaccinated against or exposed to the microbe or toxin causing the disease

Lambda Phage: A virus called a bacteriophage that infects the bacterium *E. Coli*

Metamorphosis: Some animals dramatically change physical form in stages as they develop into adults. Monarch butterfly caterpillars, for example, molt (shed their skin), form a chrysalis for protection, and finally emerge as butterflies.

Microbes: Small organisms, including bacteria, viruses, and fungi. Some are beneficial to humans and others can cause disease

Natural Selection: A natural process where individuals or groups that are best suited to their environmental conditions are more likely to survive and produce offspring

Neurons: Nerve cells

Osmosis: The movement of a substance through a membrane from one place to another to equalize chemical concentration (for example, when a solution passes through a cell membrane)

Pasteurization: A method used to partially sterilize a substance, such as dairy milk, by heating to destroy harmful pathogens while preserving nutrients and flavor

Pathogens: Certain microbes, such as specific types of bacteria, viruses, or fungi which cause disease

Penicillin: Chemical compounds made by *Penicillium* molds that can stop or slow the growth of some harmful bacteria

Phagocytosis: An important biological defense mechanism in which white blood cells called phagocytes surround and destroy foreign objects and microbes, such as bacteria

Pollination: A process in flowering plants that transfers pollen from one plant to another to allow fertilization (for example, the pollination of fruit trees by bees)

Trait: Observable physical feature, such as flower color or plant height in pea plants

REFERENCES

LAB 1

Jabr, Ferris. "How Did Insect Metamorphosis Evolve?" *Scientific American*, August 10, 2012. www. scientificamerican.com/article/ insect-metamorphosis-evolution

LAB 3

Galapagos Conservation Trust. "Darwin's Finches." galapagosconservation.org.uk/ wildlife/darwins-finches

LAB 7

"Robert Koch: Biography." Nobel Prize in Physiology or Medicine 1905. www. nobelprize.org/prizes/medicine/1905/ koch/biographical

LAB 9

"Ilya Mechnikov: Biography." Nobel Prize in Physiology or Medicine 1908. www.nobelprize.org/prizes/ medicine/1908/mechnikov/ biographical

Mackowiak, Philip A. "Recycling Metchnikoff: Probiotics, the Intestinal Microbiome and the Quest for Long Life." *Frontiers in Public Health*, 1, no. 52 (2013). doi:10.3389/fpubh.2013.00052

Norkin, Leonard. "Élie Metchnikoff: The 'Father of Innate Immunity.'" November 3, 2016. norkinvirology. wordpress.com/2016/11/03/elie-metch-nikoff-the-father-of-innate-immunity

Diagram of amoeba engulfing a particle of food by phagocytosis by Kate Taylor [CC0] Wikipedia

LAB 11

Chudler, Eric H. *Brain Lab for Kids: 52 Mind-Blowing Experiments, Models, and Activities to Explore Neuroscience*. Quarry Books, 2018.

LAB 12

Lee, Danielle N. "Diversity and Inclusion Activisms in Animal Behaviour and the ABS: A Historical View from the USA." *Animal Behaviour*, 164 (June 2020): 273–280. doi. org/10.1016/j.anbehav.2020.03.019

Britannica. "Charles Henry Turner." www.britannica.com/biography/ Charles-Henry-Turner

Zhang, Xuan "Silvia." "Insects Are Revealing How AI Can Work in Society." *VentureBeat*, September 5, 2017. venturebeat.com/2017/09/05/ insects-are-revealing-how-ai-can-work-in-society

LAB 13

Kerlin, Kat. "Grasslands More Reliable Carbon Sink Than Trees." *Science & Climate*, UC-Davis, July 9, 2018. climat-echange.ucdavis.edu/news/grasslands-more-reliable-carbon-sink-than-trees

Chase, Mary Agnes. Biography. *JSTOR* plants.jstor.org/stable/10.5555/al.ap. person.bm000001409

LAB 14

Vaughan, Carson. "The Incredible Legacy of Susan La Flesche, the First Native American to Earn a Medical Degree." *Smithsonian Magazine*, March 1, 2017. www.smithsonianmag. com/history/incredible-legacy-su-san-la-flesche-first-native-ameri-can-earn-medical-degree-180962332

LAB 15

García, María-Cristina. "Mexía de Reygades, Ynés (1870–1938)." *Texas State Historical Association: Handbook of Texas*. tshaonline.org/handbook/ online/articles/fme54

University of California, Berkeley. "Ynés Mexía collection, 1918-1966." ucjepsarchives.berkeley. edu/archon/?p=collections/findin-gaid&id=77&q=&rootcontentid=7350

Canada Journal. "Ynés Mexía: Google Doodle Honors Tenacious Mexican-American and Explorer." September 15, 2019. canadajournal.net/world/ ynes-mexia-google-doodle-honors-te-nacious-mexican-american-and-explorer-59595-2019

Smithsonian Institution. "Plant DNA Barcode Project." naturalhistory. si.edu/research/botany/research/ plant-dna-barcode-project

International Barcode of Life. "DNA Barcoding: A Tool for Specimen Identification and Species Discovery." ibol.org/about/dna-barcoding

LAB 16

"Sir Alexander Fleming: Biography." Nobel Prize in Physiology or Medicine 1945. www.nobelprize.org/prizes/ medicine/1945/fleming/biographical

LAB 17

Mangal, Mélina. *The Vast Wonder of the World: Biologist Ernest Everett Just*. Millbrook Press, 2018.

LAB 18

"Jacques Monod: Biography." Nobel Prize in Physiology or Medicine 1965. www.nobelprize.org/prizes/medicine/1965/monod/biographical

LAB 20

"Professor Esther Lederberg." WhatIsBiotechnology.org. www.whatisbiotechnology.org/index.php/people/summary/Lederberg_Esther

LAB 22

Gaunt, Sandra L. L. and Barbara B. DeWolfe. "In Memoriam: Luis Felipe Baptista, 1941–2000." *The Auk*, 118 (2), 2001: 496–499.

Mosco, Rosemary. "A Beginner's Guide to Common Bird Sounds and What They Mean." *Audoubon*, April 12, 2017. www.audubon.org/news/a-beginners-guide-common-bird-sounds-and-what-they-mean

LAB 23

"Patricia Bath: Biography." April 2, 2014. www.biography.com/scientist/patricia-bath

LAB 24

Your Wild Life. "Before They Were Scientists: Danielle N. Lee." yourwildlife.org/2014/02/before-they-were-scientists-danielle-n-lee

The Story Collider. "Danielle N. Lee: Working Twice as Hard." December 8, 2013. www.story-collider.org/stories/2016/1/4/danielle-n-lee-working-twice-as-hard

LAB 25

Boyd, Herb. "Dr. Rae Wynn-Grant, a Wildlife Specialist with an Interest in Bears." *Amsterdam News*, September 28, 2017. amsterdamnews.com/news/2017/sep/28/dr-rae-wynn-grant-wild-life-specialist-interest-bea

Dr. Rae Wynn-Grant: www.raewynn-grant.com
"Dr. Rae Wynn-Grant: Visiting Scientist." American Museum of Natural History: www.amnh.org/research/staff-directory/rae-wynn-grant

Learn, Joshua Rapp. "JWM: Translocated Horned Lizards Face New Hurdles." *The Wildlife Society*, March 6, 2020. wildlife.org/jwm-translocated-horned-lizards-face-new-hurdles

ACKNOWLEDGMENTS

This book was written and photographed during the spring and summer of 2020 amidst the COVID-19 pandemic. I am extremely grateful to all the people who labored to put this book together under extraordinary conditions.

First, I would like to thank the team at Quarry Books: acquiring editor Jonathan Simcosky, art director Heather Godin, project managers Nyle Vialet and Renae Haines, copyeditor Jenna Nelson, senior marketing director Angela Corpus, and the entire design and editing team. I am very lucky to have such a talented, supportive group to work with.

Thank you to my literary agent, Rhea Lyons whose constant positive attitude is nothing short of inspiring.

Special thanks to Dr. Danielle Lee and Dr. Rae Wynn-Grant, for allowing me to include them in the book as shining examples of modern biologists.

To photograph this book, we wore masks, kept photo shoots small, and photographed all the projects outdoors. Thank you to photographer Amber Procaccini for capturing the science projects and kids so beautifully. Thank you, Bridget, Cela, Claire, Divya, Frances, Gunnar, Haakon, Henry, Kirin, Mark, Scarlett, and Soren, for being amazing model scientists. Thank you, Kelly Anne Dalton for bringing the biologists in these pages to life with your gorgeous illustrations.

Finally, thank you to my family and friends—especially Ken, Charlie, May, and Sarah. There's no one I'd rather be stuck in a house with during a pandemic.

ABOUT THE AUTHOR

Liz Heinecke has loved science since she was old enough to inspect her first butterfly. After working in molecular biology research for ten years and getting her master's degree, Liz left the lab to kick off a new chapter in her life as a stay-at-home mom. Soon she found herself sharing her love of science with her three kids as they grew, journaling their science adventures on her online educational platform KitchenPantryScientist.com.

Her desire to spread her enthusiasm for science to others soon led to regular TV appearances, speaking engagements, and her books: *Kitchen Science Lab for Kids* (Quarry Books), *Outdoor Science Lab for Kids* (Quarry Books), *STEAM Lab for Kids* (Quarry Books), *Star Wars Maker Lab* (DK), *Kitchen Science Lab for Kids, Edible Edition* (Quarry Books), *The Kitchen Pantry Scientist: Chemistry for Kids* (Quarry Books), and "*RADIANT: The Dancer, The Scientist and a Friendship Forged in Light,*" an adult nonfiction narrative about Marie Curie and Loie Fuller (Grand Central Publishing).

Most days, you'll find Liz at home in Minnesota, writing, reading, creating science experiments, singing, playing banjo, gardening, running, and feeding hungry teenagers.

Liz graduated from Luther College with a B.A. in art and received her master's degree in bacteriology from the University of Wisconsin, Madison.

ABOUT THE PHOTOGRAPHER

Amber Procaccini is a commercial and editorial photographer based in Minneapolis, Minnesota. She specializes in photographing kids, babies, food, and travel, and her passion for photography almost equals her passion for finding the perfect taco.

Amber met Liz while photographing her first book, *Kitchen Science Lab for Kids,* and she knew they'd make a great team when they bonded over cornichons, pate, and brie. When Amber isn't photographing eye-rolling tweens or making cheeseburgers look mouthwatering, she and her husband love to travel and enjoy new adventures together.

ABOUT THE ILLUSTRATOR

Kelly Anne Dalton is a professional artist and illustrator living in the wild mountains of Montana. Working from her charming 1920s studio, Kelly Anne loves creating a wide range of work from children's books to decorative greeting cards and gifts. Growing up with a biologist for a mother, Kelly has had an appreciation for science and nature her entire life and because of that she enjoyed creating the portraits for this book. When not drawing, Kelly Anne can be found trail running in the forest, playing with her dogs, and adventuring with her husband.

INDEX